The Easter Passage

The RCIA Experience

Mary Pierre Ellebracht, CPPS

WINSTON PRESS

Cover photo: Cyril A. Reilly

Excerpts from *The Jerusalem Bible,* copyright © 1966 by
Darton, Longman & Todd, Ltd. and Doubleday and
Company, Inc., used by permission of the publisher.

Portions of Chapter 4 appeared originally in a somewhat
different form as "The Eucharistic Prayer: Celebrating Our
Mutuality as God's Holy People" in *Emmanuel* 87 (1981), pp.
217-224. Used with permission.

Scripture texts used in this work are taken from the *New
American Bible* and the *Lectionary for Mass,* © 1970, by the
Confraternity of Christian Doctrine, Washington, D.C., and
are used by permission of the copyright owner. All rights
reserved.

Excerpts from the English translation of *Lectionary for Mass,*
© 1969, International Committee on English in the Liturgy,
Inc. (ICEL); excerpts from the English translation of *The
Roman Missal,* © 1973, ICEL; excerpts from the English
translation from the *Rite of Christian Initiation of Adults,* ©
1974, ICEL. Used by permission. All rights reserved.

Library of Congress Catalog Card Number: 82-51160

ISBN: 0-86683-693-4

Printed in the United States of America

5   4   3   2   1

Winston Press, Inc.
430 Oak Grove
Minneapolis, Minnesota 55403

CONTENTS

PREFACE

This book has been long in the making. During my religious formation in the 1930s, the late Martin B. Hellriegel introduced me to Odo Casel's insights into the liturgical mysteries. Hellriegel's teaching could be considered the beginning of this book's Period of Catechumenate. Michael Mathis, CSC, and especially Professor Cornelius A. Bouman of Nijmegen, Holland, continued that Catechumenate and deepened my liturgical education during that time.

Cultural changes such as the advances in rapid communication, and the documents of Vatican Council II, and Ignatian retreat experiences all led me into deeper conversion and could be termed the book's Period of Purification and Enlightenment. The suggestion of Sister Bernarda Bockrath, CPPS, that I write the book, and the understanding support of Gil Ostdeik, OFM, could be called the book's actual Initiation.

As I reflect now on the entire process, I experience a kind of Mystagogia, and so a series of further grateful acknowledgments are in order. I am grateful to Dr. Ralph Keifer for recognizing that *The Easter Passage: The RCIA Experience* will be a help to the American Church as it seeks to implement the Rite of Christian Initiation of Adults (RCIA), and I deeply appreciate his willingness to write the Foreword. I am grateful to Barbara Groneck, who with constant encouragement spent hours lovingly typing copy from tangled rough drafts, and to Sr. Anthony Naes, CPPS, who typed the copy as devotedly as though it were her own.

In all of this I witness to the providence of God within my own CPPS community.

September 12, 1982
The anniversary of my entry
into Christ Life as Mildred Ellebracht

FOREWORD

In terms of their potential for the renewal of the life and prayer of the Church, three liturgical reforms initiated by the Second Vatican Council stand out above all others: the restoration of the Liturgy of the Word, the reformed Lectionary with its cycles of readings, and the restored Rite for the Christian Initiation of Adults. These reforms represent far more than mere ceremonial revision or improvement of text. In many ways, they constitute a liturgical embodiment of the Council's hope and vision. Several aspirations were at the heart of the Council's deliberations, and they found full voice in some of its most significant documents, especially the Dogmatic Constitution on the Church *(Lumen Gentium)* and the Pastoral Constitution on the Church in the Modern World *(Gaudium et Spes)*. Pope John XXIII announced the Council as representing a hope for Christian unity, and that hope shaped many of its documents. At the heart of that hope was a concern for the Christian mission in our world; and the vision of the Council was for a church renewed, where all believers would understand themselves as the bearers of that mission. The dramatic reopening of the Word in liturgy and lectionary is not only a matter of taking the critique of the Reformers with somewhat belated seriousness. It is also a challenge to recover our biblical roots, to understand ourselves once again as a people with a common mission.

That reopening of the Word to Catholics has in fact turned out to be one of the major ecumenical achievements of our time. Not only have we begun to rediscover the Scriptures, but we also now share a common lectionary with other major churches. But the possibilities extend beyond this important achievement. The reopening of the treasures of the Word constitutes a call to rediscover for our own time the mystery of God working among us as a people—a call especially to take ourselves seriously as a people who announce that mystery as it finds its center and culmination in the death and resurrection of Jesus Christ and the sending of the Spirit. In some significant departures from attitudes of recent centuries, the Council saw the adult laity as significant agents of that good news. A church which is essentially constituted of adult hearers and bearers of the Word needs to know the shape and scope of their own gift and mission if they are to take hold of it as their own. We need the witness of adult lay faith in the Church, for we need to know what it looks like to take hold of and live that faith in our own world. This is the purpose of the process known as adult initiation. The process by which adults' new faith takes shape within the life of the Church is celebrated liturgically so that an adult laity may have the benefit of the witness of adult laity, in the liturgy as well as outside of it.

The Christian initiation of an adult is not only, and perhaps not primarily, for the benefit of the new believer: it is also, and perhaps primarily, for the benefit of the whole Church, a public witness so that those coming to faith may call all of us to deeper and wider faith. There is thus an intimate, even integral, connection between the restoration of the Word and the Christian initiation of adults. Together, they both tell us who we are and call us to own up to it. All three—Liturgy of the Word, Lectionary, and the Rite for the Christian Initiation of Adults—find their consummation in the celebration of the Lenten and Easter Seasons. The God who brings life out of death is celebrated from the ashes of Lent's beginning to the pentecostal fire of the great and last day of the Easter Season. By the word of Scripture and the Easter sacraments for adults, we are brought to know anew what it is to proclaim Jesus Christ dead and risen and alive among us in the Spirit.

Sister Ellebracht has produced a work which interweaves the scriptural message with the celebration of the Easter sacraments. Nothing could be more timely, nor more needed. If we are to recover the fulness of our biblical heritage, we must perceive the essential relationship between word and sacrament that is at the heart of our own tradition. Sister Ellebracht provides important pointers to a recovery of our own heritage for our own time.

Ralph Keifer

INTRODUCTION

Planted deep within the human heart is the desire to be personally united with God, our merciful savior, tender lover, and compassionate father. The realization that we can only gradually satisfy this desire is just as deep within us. Hence being "on the way" is an appropriate image for expressing this human condition. It is an image we find particularly—though not exclusively—in the Judeo-Christian tradition to express both moral and religious progress. For God's people in the Old Testament, the image of "the way" not only included movement and progress; it also symbolized the experience of passage from one state to another, and essentially different, state. The primary example of this experience is the Israelites' passage through the Red Sea—symbolic of their liberation from slavery and their movement into freedom (Exod. 14:14-31). Jesus, in his turn, gave this image its richest meaning when he revealed himself to be *the Way* to union with the Father. "I am the way, and the truth, and the life; no one comes to the Father but through me" (John 14:6).[1] Jesus became and is forever the only way into the holy of holies (Heb. 9:8).

The earliest Christians realized that they were followers of the Way (Acts 9:2; 18:25; 19:9; 22:4; 24:14). They knew that people need time to be converted and that conversion itself is ever ongoing. Christians, very early, devised a period of preparation for the initiation of new members. This period of preparation, known as the catechumenate, had developed by the middle of the fourth century. It lasted for three years or more. Since it was a time of preparation intended to lead to conversion, the catechesis given was directed not primarily to the intellect but toward moral conversion and personal commitment to Christ in the Church. The entire community was involved in the catechumenate process, which in turn became a vehicle of preparation for the faithful as well. In patristic literature we find references to the time of preparation for initiation as Quadragesima or the Forty Days, the time of celebration as Triduum, and the time of joyful reflection as the Fifty Days.[2]

These seasons have never been lost in the Church, not even when, for many complex reasons, the adult catechumenate all but disappeared. True, the length of the period of Lent has been altered several times in Lent's long history; the pervading Christian sentiment during the celebration of the Triduum shifted from entry into the Paschal Mystery to devotion to it and back again; and the sequence and number of scripture readings in the liturgies was altered periodically. Nevertheless, through all these shiftings, the seasons of Lent, Triduum, and Easter Time remained as periods of initiation and renewal marked by special prayer, penance, more frequent reception of the sacraments, and more elaborate celebration.

Because conversion/initiation should continue throughout every Christian's life, these periods are important to the entire body of the Church and not only to those who are seeking admission as new members. The *Constitution on the Sacred Liturgy* called for a greater use of the baptismal and penitential elements proper to the Season of Lent (#109)[3] and also directed that "the catechumenate for adults, comprising several distinct steps, is to be restored. . ." (L#64). Then the RCIA itself was promulgated in 1972.[4]

Many pastors, liturgists, and other perceptive Christians have praised this rite. It begins with a period of inquiry and evangelization, followed by a period of catechesis called catechumenate. An intensive period of purification and enlightenment takes place during the season of Lent. The actual celebration of the initiation sacraments happens during the Triduum at the Easter Vigil. Finally, a period called Mystagogia follows during the Easter season. Aidan Kavanagh hailed it with these words of hope: "It is a practicable vision of what the Church is and can become through the continuing renewal process of evangelization, conversion, catechesis, and the Paschal sacraments of Christian initiation."[5] The Introduction to the Rite states:

> The rite of initiation is suited to the spiritual journey of adults, which varies according to the many forms of God's grace, the free cooperation of the individuals, the action of the Church, and the circumstances of time and place. (RCIA #5)

The RCIA is not an entirely new rite, but it does represent a way of implementing something imbedded deep in the sensitivity of the Church: that initiation and renewal are essential to the process of growth in Christ.

The objective of this book is not to study the liturgical prescriptions of Lent-Triduum-Easter, but to help readers contemplate, i.e., take a long loving look at, our Father's compassionate plan to save us and, through this reflection, to help them enter more fully into that plan. The theological reflection is by no means exhaustive; in fact, it approaches more closely what might be called taking an appreciative look at what we have experienced and at how we have entered into the Mystery of Christ in his own passage to the Father. This kind of reflection will be growth-producing to the extent that we are in touch with our own deepest desires. When we are open in this way, we will come to *know* the life force and love power that touches us during the moments of intensity we name rituals.

Regarding initiation, we share the misgivings voiced by Ralph Keifer when he observed that new members can be partially assimilated into the Church but not really initiated into it because, at present, the Church has no way of acting as a community.[6] That is, we seem unable, either individually or communally, to name and voice the realities targeted by our feelings. This is so because many persons are either psychically unable to name their feelings or are afraid to voice them. If this is difficult on the psychic level, it is even more difficult to express faith experiences with clarity and enthusiasm.

In response to this difficulty, then, this book attempts to demonstrate how various scripture passages used in the Lent-Triduum-Easter liturgies actually do touch our lives (i.e., do name and express our faith experiences) in meaningful ways. By putting us in contact with the human movements within us, *The Easter Passage* invites us to recognize the human-divine content of our faith experiences, to witness to them, and to encourage others to share them. Thus this book will serve catechists, sponsors, catechumens, and other Christians interested in sharing the apostolic mission of the Church. It will also help those who are themselves seeking to live their life-in-Christ more fully and are "teaching" liturgy to others.

Chapter 1 is a lead-in to the entire work and speaks of *how* we enter into God's plan. It deals, in the first place, with how God's Spirit-filled Word helps us encounter God in the divine-human dialogue. A brief discussion follows concerning the shape this encounter takes in the Church; this discussion shows that we can find the structures of such (liturgical) encounters in the earliest Church accounts. Chapter 1 also emphasizes that the structures have not been imposed on us but have been formed from the vitality generated in each meeting between God and his people.

Chapters 2 and 3 deal with the mystery celebrated during the successive Sundays of Lent. This mystery is that of being *chosen* by God and called along the way of the successive steps in the process of initiation and renewal. The Sixth Sunday, Passion (Palm) Sunday, celebrates both the climax and the source of the conversion process, viz., Christ's saving death. The solemnities of the Holy Triduum make up the content of Chapter 4. These include the celebration of the Lord's Supper, the Sacred Passion, the long silent Saturday, the Great Vigil, and Easter Sunday.[7] Chapter 5 contains reflections on Easter Time as the season of the postbaptismal catechesis or the Mystagogia. Finally, a very brief summary and reflection comprise the Epilogue.

The Easter Passage: The RCIA Experience aims to enable readers to trace the action of God in their lives, to recognize this divine initiative in the Word of God proclaimed and responded to in succeeding liturgical celebrations, and finally, to participate in appropriate ritual behaviors which will both express and intensify their response to God. Throughout this book we work from the assumption that rituals cannot be explained but that, like symbols, they must be discovered.

Before proceeding any further, a brief comment on the meaning of two words that occur frequently in this work seems necessary. Much of the meaning of the text depends upon the way these words are used and understood. The first of these is *mystery*.[8] On the whole, the word is employed to mean the presence and action of Christ the Lord among us, e.g., "Mystery of Christ." Even when it is thus used, however, the word *mystery* also carries ritual overtones whenever it is employed in the liturgy. Used in this cultic sense, the word means the inner effect, along with the external form, of the rite being celebrated. Finally, the text uses the word to refer to the "liturgical mystery" or the particular day or season of the year which memorializes a work of the Savior. It is in this last sense that the term *the Paschal Mystery*— which generally means Christ's death and resurrection—designates the Christian assembly's total celebration of Lent, Triduum, and Easter Time. In every case, the term *mystery* connotes "a divine-human reality" that we share.

The second word is *know*. We come to know this divine-human reality in a faith experience. This volume, for the most part, uses the word *know*, in its biblical sense, where it stands for more than, but does not exclude, "intellectual awareness" or "being in possession of facts." Biblically, the term *know* refers to experience—physical, psychological and spiritual, as well as intellectual; it includes both the rational and the numerous nonrational ways of knowing: for example, through images, symbols, stories, dreams, visions, sex, peace, to name a few. All these ways of knowing move toward giving us personal certainty. Thus, for example, when the text says that we *know* the Lord is calling us to conversion, we are dealing with a faith reality that catches us up into itself and illumines the intellectual, the physical, the psychological, and the spiritual levels of our being.

We also need to mention two further aspects of our approach to the mysteries treated in this work. First, we view the human person not piecemeal but as a unity; and second, we regard Christian initiation and renewal as ongoing realities.

Since *The Easter Passage* views the human person as an integrated phenomenon, when the text says that the successive stages of our desire to be special to a significant other are the foundation upon which rests our coming to *know* in faith that we are the chosen ones, the beloved of God, it is not merely speaking of a faith reality in the jargon of modern psychology. Rather, it is affirming that God saves us as *whole* persons. We can expect, then, that the dynamism engendered within human dialogue will become the symbol of the powerful presence of the Spirit in the dialogue of the Liturgy of the Word as well as in the dialogue that introduces the Eucharistic Prayer. In fact, that dynamism is part of salvation.

To understand how Christian initiation and renewal are growing realities, we must first clarify the meaning of three more key words and their derivatives: *intuitive, transcendent,* and *contemplative.*

The seed serves as a useful analogy to describe the growth of the divine life within us. When the seed falls into the ground, it has within it the potential to grow, but it cannot cause this growth. When the conditions of the soil and the atmosphere are right, the seed *knows* a kind of urge to grow. If the seed could think and choose, it would have to decide either to rot or to allow its inner urge for growth to take it above the ground and into a state of its own being of which it has no previous experience.

Intuitive. The text employs the phrase *to know intuitively* to refer to that first vague but persistent human awareness that something new is straining to come into being, that growth is beginning. For the human person, the call to growth is personal, and it comes from God. This call means letting go, relinquishing, losing the life we know at the present time.

Transcendent. This call means *transcending* ourselves; it involves allowing ourselves to be lured into a new relationship and into a wholly new condition of existence, a state radically *transcending* our current experience. Because it involves an entirely new way of relating and a whole new meaning for our lives, the risk entailed in saying yes to God is total, but the new, *transcendent* life is rich and joy-filled.

Contemplative. Since we can do nothing to initiate such growth, all we can do at first is *contemplate* it when it happens. As we acknowledge it and ponder it in our hearts, we are enabled both to affirm it and to praise God gratefully for it in celebration. Because growth takes place according to a recognizable pattern, we can trace its progress through the entire journey into faith. The parameters of this journey can be set—though not fixed—in the Church's celebration of Lent, Triduum, and Easter Time.

In conclusion, *The Easter Passage* attempts to demonstrate how the Paschal Mystery directs our life—the new life we enter by conversion. This book seeks to shed light on the life stream that flows through the Church's listening and responding to the Word of God, through its celebrations of the RCIA rituals during Lent, and through its Sunday celebrations of Eucharist as it journeys through Lent, Triduum, and Easter Time. This study seeks throughout to hold both sides of the Paschal Mystery in tension.[9] It demonstrates that the paschal lamb has to be slain again and again in the painful relinquishments demanded by growth; at the same time, it points out how each passage across a dangerous boundary leads to the new life of unsuspected intimacy with God in Christ.

It does not bypass the Christian's day-to-day living nor overlook the human struggle to become fully integrated persons. On the contrary, *The Easter Passage* offers a contemplative guide to catechumen and faithful alike as they strive to enter into God's saving plan made present in the celebrations of the sacred liturgy.

Notes

1. *The New American Bible,* © 1970, Confraternity of Christian Doctrine, Washington, D.C. All further quotations taken from this translation will be identified as NAB.
2. See Patrick Regan, OSB, "The Three Days and the Forty Days," *Worship* 54 (January 1980):2-18.
3. *Constitution on the Sacred Liturgy,* Second Vatican Council (Collegeville, Minn.: Liturgical Press, 1963), #109. Further references to this document will be marked as "L" plus the paragraph number.
4. *Rite of Christian Initiation of Adults,* © 1974, the International Committee on English in the Liturgy. All further quotations from this text will be identified as RCIA with the article number.
5. Aidan Kavanagh, "The Shape of Baptism," in *The Rite of Christian Initiation* (New York: Pueblo Publishing Co., 1978), p. 127.
6. Ralph Keifer, "Christian Initiation: The State of the Question," in *Made, not Born* (Notre Dame: University of Notre Dame Press, 1976), p. 142.
7. See this arrangement and also some of its ambiguities in *Calendarium Romanum,* Editio Typica, Typis Polyglottis Vaticanis, 1969.
8. See Mary P. Ellebracht, CPPS, *Remarks on the Vocabulary of the Ancient Orations in the Missale Romanum* (Nijmegen: Dekker en Van de Vegt, 1963), pp. 67-71, for a treatment of this word in the cultic sense and also for a bibliography of other works on this subject.
9. See Christine Mohrmann, "Pascha, Passio, Transitus," in *Etudes sur le Latin des Chrétiens,* vol. 1 (Rome: Edizioni di Storia E Letteratura, 1958), pp. 205-222, particularly pp. 206 and 222.

1

GOD SO LOVED THE WORLD

The Letter to the Ephesians begins with a hymn of praise to the God who devised a merciful plan to bring the entire universe into a marvelous unity. This unity has been, and is being, achieved in Christ Jesus.

> Praised be the God and Father of our Lord Jesus Christ, who has bestowed on us in Christ every spiritual blessing in the heavens! God chose us in him before the world began, to be holy and blameless in his sight, to be full of love; he likewise predestined us through Christ Jesus to be his adopted sons—such was his will and pleasure—that all might praise the glorious favor he has bestowed on us in his beloved. (Eph. 1:3-6 NAB)

We may look upon creation as the first stage of God's design for humankind. In fact, the first creation story (Gen. 1:1-2:4a) indicates that we are destined for intimacy with God, the same intimacy mentioned in the prayer of Jesus before his death:

> Eternal life is this: to know you the only true God, and him whom you have sent, Jesus Christ. (John 17:3 NAB)[1]

The text of Genesis first reveals this intimacy in the words "Let us make man in our image, after our likeness" (Gen. 1:26 NAB). The second creation account (Gen. 2:4b-25) reveals it even more dramatically: "the LORD God formed man out of the clay of the ground and blew into his nostrils the breath of life, and so man became a living being" (Gen. 2:7 NAB). Both accounts indicate the faith awareness of their authors, viz., the authors *knew* that human beings were capable of entering into a relationship of friendship and intimacy with God.

We too possess this faith awareness. Furthermore, we are equally aware that by sin we have forfeited our destiny to have God walk with us in the garden (Gen. 3:8-10). With the authors of those early writings, we realize how radically helpless we are to restore ourselves to our pristine state. There seems to be an impasse between God and us; and upon reflection we come to understand that unredeemed human beings are indeed fettered and helpless.

We also *know* that from the beginning God's plan includes sending the Son to redeem us: God " . . . chose us in him (Christ) before the world began. . . ." (Eph. 1:4 NAB). Numerous early Christian prayers succinctly express their authors' same faith awareness. For example, the Opening Prayer of December 25, in the *Sacramentary of Verona*, says:[2] "O God, you have marvelously created human beings and have made them even more wonderful by your act of redemption."[3] In Christian liturgical Latin the word *mirabiliter,* "marvelously," connotes more than "wonderful" or "happily out of the ordinary." It contains within it the sense of "something accomplished by divine power" and therefore "something which surpasses *all* human expectation." A second and perhaps even more striking example of Christian reflection that from the beginning God's merciful plan for us included redemption as well as creation may be found in the Easter Proclamation or *Exsultet:*

What good would life have been to us,
    had Christ not come as our Redeemer?
Father, how wonderful your care for us!
    How boundless your merciful love!
    To ransom a slave
    you gave away your Son.[4]

Appreciating the depth of the mystery of both creation and redemption hinges upon our enjoyment of an interpersonal relationship with God. We are not destined to be passive receivers of gifts from God. Rather, we are meant to enter into *dialogue* with God and thus enjoy *personal* encounter with the divine. God always remains the beloved who takes the initiative and woos the members of the human family into covenant relationship with himself. God is our Emmanuel always dynamically present to us, always acting on our behalf. When in the fullness of time God sent his beloved Son to be the ultimate expression of divine love, God revealed his choice to express divine compassion in *human* terms.

Jesus announced that he was the Messiah sent to redeem humankind, and he spoke with authority, with inner personal creative power. He attracted persons at the deepest level of their beings and called them to inner conversion. We see this in his encounters with the alienated—for example, with the woman in the house of the Pharisee, with the tax collectors, and with the Samaritan woman. In every case, Jesus was able to help the individual person recognize that she or he was a lover, albeit an unfaithful one at times.

If this was true of Jesus in his mortal life, we can expect it to be even more true as he reigns at the right hand of the Father, interceding for us. Being Messiah to sinful human beings implies a change not in God, but in *human* hearts. However, we sinful human beings only gradually realize that we are lovers at heart. To say yes to the advances of love we must radically change our attitudes and life-style. Maturity comes slowly, and only the spiritually mature can commit themselves to a love bond. Only the spiritually mature can know the meaning of the words of the fourth reading of the Easter Vigil: "He who has become your husband is your Maker" (Isa. 54:5 NAB).

The Father gave Jesus the mission of offering us a share in the mutuality that Jesus enjoyed with God: " . . . he likewise predestined us through Christ to be adopted sons" (Eph. 1:5 NAB). Jesus did this by taking our sins upon himself (see 1 Pet. 2:24). His crucifixion was not a matter of placating an angry Father who had been holding out against sinful children; nor was it a sentimental, tear-jerking episode designed to stir up emotions and to shame us into changing our behavior. No, Christ's saving act was destined to heal us in our deepest hearts, i.e., at the center of our being where we say "I am." However incomprehensible it may seem to us, the ability to relate to God personally depends on our knowing that we have been forgiven.[5] When we behold the Crucified One, God enables us in faith to abandon the fear that hinders us from accepting the unconditional acceptance that God offers us. Jesus crucified enables us to give up the lie that forces us to look upon God as our accuser.[6]

In this book we are seeking to uncover the saving plan of God as it is experienced in the Church today. In the celebration of the liturgy, the Church does "apply him [Christ], and what he was and is to the present."[7] The sacred action of worship leads us to find meaning in our lives in terms of Christ's passing from death to newness of life, his Easter passage. He is always the definitive expression of the Father's compassionate concern and the fulfillment of God's saving plan for us.

Thus, this work plans to lead readers to a long, loving look at the human-divine life pulsating within the liturgical structures that today we call the Forty Days of Lent, the Sacred Triduum, and Easter Time.[8]

God's Saving Plan Grows from Within

We will look at the unfolding of God's saving plan from two viewpoints. First we will focus on the inner movement by which the Word of God becomes a present reality for us human beings, an event that makes an essential difference in our lives. Then we will trace the pattern of growth this inner vitality has followed, the pattern that has become the structure supporting the very life that forms it.

The Word of God Becomes a Present Reality

Since God deals with human beings in accordance with their freedom, God's plan is essentially dialogic. For this reason it may be well to consider some basic analogues that focus our attention more closely upon the inner movement of the faith life that this divine-human dialogue engenders. It will be helpful to reflect on how words affect us in our everyday lives and to recall occasions when words have truly become events for us. For example, words such as "Come to our house for dinner sometime," or "I'll make time for you," or "Will you marry me?" tend to be creative. They become events. Words of love and concern have the greatest impact on us because they establish rapport and provide us with an absolutely indispensable ingredient in our lives: relationships. Moreover, they offer us something we could never provide for ourselves.

Another helpful analogue is memory. Memory gives continuity to our lives and enables us to enter more happily into the everlasting plan of salvation. Events of our lives remain within our memory, and whenever we recall them they become present to us.

To recognize the event-making, memory-evoking power in the Word of God, we can look again at how the Old Testament viewed God's Word as creative.[9] "By the word of the LORD the heavens were made" (Ps. 33:6 NAB). The repetition of the phrase "and God said" in the first creation story provides another instance for reflection on the creative power of the divine Word. Again, the Word of God at Mount Sinai called forth from God's people their believing answer: "Everything the LORD has said, we will do" (Exod. 19:8 NAB). The mutuality (dialogue) thus created between God and Israel constituted the Covenant; the Word became event. The Word of God to Mary and her word of acceptance (dialogue) brought the Word of God to earth in human form: The Word became flesh.

These examples bring us to the next step in the process of divine Word becoming present reality: the point where the Word of God elicits a response from a human partner and thus initiates a divine-human dialogue. The dynamism within such dialogue creates the life of faith within us. And this dynamism is the power of the Holy Spirit. The event recorded in the second chapter of the Acts of the Apostles illustrates this point. In this account, the first thing we notice is that the community is assembled in prayer and is therefore engaged in dialogue with God. The presence and power of the Spirit become singularly evident in the wind and the tongues of fire. Those gathered in the upper room then respond to the Spirit's presence and complete the dialogue by making "bold proclamations as the Spirit prompted them" (Acts 2:4 NAB).[10]

What is present within the memory of the entire community by the power of the Spirit, Peter makes public. As he recounts the sequence of events that led to the death and rising of Jesus, Peter is doing more than narrating the raw historical data. He is proclaiming what he himself experiences, for Peter has not only lived through that sequence; he also *knows* that it provided him with a close encounter with Christ. This latter reality is still alive within him. Thus the conscious content of Peter's message is nothing short of Christ himself in his passing from death to new life.[11] Peter's word is an expression of faith; he knows that he has also passed from death to new life with Christ. Therefore Peter is memorializing the passover of Jesus. Speaking in the power of the Spirit—without whom we are unable to say "Jesus is Lord"—Peter is making *anamnesis,* i.e., proclaiming what is present in his memory.

Peter explains the inner meaning of his message when he says, "God has made both Lord and Messiah this Jesus whom you crucified" (Acts 2:36 NAB). In telling the story he is making present, "present-ing,"[12] God's saving action that exists eternally in God's love and concern. This love has reached a definitive fullness in the life, death, and resurrection of Jesus and finds a new presence and mode of efficacy in the heart of the crowd gathered for the Pentecost festival as they begin to be converted.

The Word of God heard by the crowd gathered around "the house where they were seated" (Acts 2:2 NAB) exists in Peter's word of faith. Its source is the Holy Spirit, active in Peter and the others, and its conscious content is Christ in his saving death and resurrection. That is why it comes with power. It impels the listeners to ask, "What must we do?" At this point the Word becomes "good news" or *kerygma,* and it moves the hearts of the listeners to repentance *(metanoia)* and conversion. Conversion calls us to become what we most desire, to become our best selves, for it opens the way to intimacy with God within the community of those God has chosen.

It is of the utmost importance that we maintain a vivid awareness of the profound meaning of the following terms when we use them or read them: (1) *kerygma,* the Word of God, becomes "good news" for us, because it is God's personal bid for closer intimacy with us; (2) *epiclesis* ("a calling upon" or "a calling over here") means our recognition of the active, intimate power of the Holy Spirit; (3) *anamnesis* ("to remember") means our making present God's saving deeds in word and sacrament. When words become technical terms, as these have, there is a danger that they may conceal more than they reveal of the throbbing life force which they mean to designate.

Although we do in fact find these terms most frequently used to designate aspects of the official worship or liturgy, we cannot and do not confine their use to the liturgy alone. The power inherent in the Word of God is released whenever God chooses to dialogue with us and we respond, whether in communal celebration or in individual contemplation. In the back-and-forth movement of such dialogue, the events of our lives get reinterpreted in light of the life, death, and resurrection of Christ. In contemplation we also discover the meaning of our lives today, even as Peter's audience did, and we are enabled "to orient them to the contemporary plan of salvation in the present-day history."[13] In this way we come to know intimately that what is happening in our lives is shaped by the events of Jesus' life, and that Jesus' story becomes our story.

A remark concerning adaptation may be helpful here. If we wish our own anamnesis of God's action to become kerygma for others, we must shape the proclamation of our believing response to the circumstances of our audience. Again, the Acts of the Apostles affords us an excellent example. In chapter ten we find the sermon given by Peter in the house of Cornelius. A number of the details of this sermon differ from the actual event recorded in chapter two. In his anamnesis, Peter adapts his remarks in order to allow the event to be kerygma for his audience. Thus he could later say unequivocally: "God was giving them the same gift he gave us when we first believed" (Acts 11:17 NAB).

We have seen how members of the early Church received the Word of God by the inner power of the Holy Spirit. Such acceptance caused radical change in the persons who received the Word in this way. In the first centuries such persons were called "faithful"; perhaps "faith-filled" is the more usual term today. So today when we, the faithful, proclaim the deed that God has accomplished in us, we tell the story. We outwardly express what is present in our lives and in our memory. In that expression we invite others to accept God's merciful action. In other words, we initiate them into Christ's Paschal Mystery.

The Structure of Our Faith Journey: The Shape of Our Response

We turn now to a consideration of the pattern of growth that the life of faith exhibits. The eternal life present to and in the Christian body through the Word of God has its own identifying characteristics. Like any other living organism—be it an elephant or a snail, a strawberry or an oak tree—Christian life builds its life-support system from within.

A distinguishing characteristic of this divine-human body is that it is a *worshiping* community. This was true of the people of God in the Old Testament, and it is true of the new people of God, the Church.[14] The inner vitality within the Church today is engendered by the mutuality among the members with and in Christ. This mutuality was made possible by Jesus Christ in his Paschal Mystery, in his Easter passage. The Spirit he sent from the Father is its bonding force. Human mutuality, then, becomes the symbol of the life of the Spirit. As such, human mutuality both partakes of and initiates the reality it signifies. As a faith symbol, it bears the vitality that makes the Holy Spirit the bonding or the soul of the Mystical Body, i.e., the source of its identity and its energy to say, "I am."

Once again, chapter two of Acts gives us evidence of the sequence of steps that led up to the earliest recorded *act* of initiating new members into the community of believers. We note the following stages in the process: (1) faith witness, or the preaching of the apostles; (2) questioning by those who are addressed; (3) the call to repentance; (4) baptism; (5) receiving the Holy Spirit. The result of the process: "Some three thousand were added that day" (Acts 2:41 NAB). A new community was born. Acts 2:42-47 even provides us with a description of the life-style of the newly formed community.

It is not surprising that documents containing source material on the initiation of new members into the Christian community indicate that the initiation process followed the pattern outlined in Acts 2.[15] Throughout the course of history some discrepancies crept into the process, certain of its parts became extended out of proportion, and others were reduced or were lost completely. While we will leave that history to others, we do want to call attention to the similarity between what we find in Acts and the format of the *Rite of Christian Initiation of Adults* (RCIA).[16]

Before we go into a detailed comparison, however, we should recall what this book seeks to accomplish. The primary aim of this work is to put readers in touch with the life that courses through the seasons of the Church Year from the beginning of Lent to the completion of the Fifty Days, or Pentecost. Getting in touch with the divine life-content includes involvement in the praise and thanks that the celebration of these seasons entail. When we, the faithful, so involve ourselves, our witness not only renews us; it also calls others to a believing

Acts 2		
Peter's sermon and faith-witness	"What are we to do?" (Acts 2:37)	"Reform and be baptized, . . .

RCIA				
			Catechumenate	
Period of Evangelization/ Precatechumenate	Rite of Becoming a Catechumen		Period of complete catechesis	Rite of Enrollment—Election
The hearts of inquirers are opened by the Holy Spirit that they might believe and be converted to the Lord. (See RCIA #9.)			Various rites of exorcism and signings	

response. In other words, therefore, we celebrate Lent, Triduum, and Easter Time as seasons of Christian initiation and renewal. We cannot repeat too often that the inner dialogue with God is what we desire and celebrate. Since this dialogue takes place within human history, we have to be concerned with the human (liturgical) structures that enflesh the dialogue and also support it.

When we compare the stages of conversion found in the second chapter of Acts with the stages outlined in the RCIA, their similarity is striking. We could outline those stages roughly as seen below:

that your sins may be forgiven. . . ." (Acts 2:38)	Be baptized; receive the Holy Spirit.	Three thousand were added: devoted themselves to apostolic teaching, common life, breaking of bread prayers. (See Acts 2:41-47.)
Catechumenate Period of purification and enlightenment Lent is a memorial of or a preparation for baptism Scrutinies	Sacraments of Initiation	Period of mystagogia Receiving sacraments, works of charity, neophytes and faithful move forward together. (See RCIA #37.)

The faith witness that was Peter's sermon parallels the RCIA's "Period of Evangelization and Precatechumenate." As in Peter's time, witnessing to the message of salvation in our day is done in the Spirit's power. Our witnessing motivates our hearers to ask, in substance, "What must we do?" Since the risen Lord in the Spirit is also the sharing source of the modern evangelizer's (our) act of faith, we can expect "those who are not yet Christians, their hearts opened by the Holy Spirit, [to] believe and be freely converted to the Lord" (RCIA #9). Being converted to the Lord is termed being "called away from sin and drawn toward the mystery of God's love" (RCIA #10).

In Acts, the people's "What must we do?" is answered by Peter's admonition to repent and seek baptism for the forgiveness of sins (Acts 2:38). Today the RCIA provides a structure for such a response in its "Rite of Becoming a Catechumen." This rite celebrates initial conversion and supports further conversion. The reform required by the revelation of God's love, which was more primitive and general in Peter's answer, has now come to be supported by rites and further celebrations (RCIA #19).

The process of conversion and preparation for baptism sometimes extends as long as three years or more. However, it culminates in the season of Lent. During this season, significant celebrations support further conversion. "The time of purification and enlightenment or illumination of the catechumens customarily coincides with Lent; both in its liturgy and in its liturgical catechesis, Lent is a memorial or a preparation for baptism and a time of penance" (RCIA #21). This significant statement reveals the inner vitality of Lent to be precisely the preparation for baptism or the making present (renewal) of this sacrament in the faithful in a way that produces further conversion. What seemed to have taken place in Jerusalem in a space of a single day (Pentecost day) has now blossomed into the six weeks of Lent—a season of newness of life. On three of the lenten Sundays—that of the Samaritan Woman (Third Sunday), that of the Man Born Blind (Fourth Sunday), and that of Lazarus (Fifth Sunday)—the liturgy helps us live through the process of conversion in slow motion, as it were, and to experience anew each of its vital movements. Passion Sunday is the climax of the six weeks of Lent. It also leads us into the Triduum, our ritual celebration of the message that Peter proclaimed: the death of Jesus and his becoming Lord and Christ. Right at the heart of the Sacred Triduum—as its high point and most intense moment—we celebrate the sacraments of initiation. In this way, Christian initiation and renewal constitute our Easter passage now.

In the course of his sermon, Peter told his hearers: "It was to you and your children that the promise was made, and to all those still far off whom the Lord our God calls" (Acts 2:39 NAB). Not only was that *promise* fulfilled in the historical happenings of the first century; it is being fulfilled today in our sacramental celebrations and in the happenings of our everyday lives. The sacramental celebrations par excellence take place during Triduum, and in particular at the Easter Vigil when those who accept the message celebrate the Easter passage and are added to the number of Christians. This great celebration constitutes in our time the same work of salvation—Christ's death and resurrection—that Peter's words actualized in Jerusalem.

Since all new life is fragile and tender, we must carefully protect and nurture it. This nurturing takes place in the celebration of Easter Time. Over and over again throughout the Fifty Days, we celebrate the presence of the risen Lord. During this time

> the community and the neophytes move forward together, meditating on the Gospel, sharing in the eucharist, and performing works of charity. In this way they understand the paschal mystery more fully and bring it into their lives more and more. (RCIA #37)

The following excellently summarizes Christian life as symbolized in the fifty days (Easter Time):

> The Fifty Days symbolize the era in which, by the release of the Spirit, this one true feast, Christ, is inserted into the present world to be shared by all who believe the Good News . . . Christ is actualized or made full as a person precisely by drawing believers into his own new humanity. . . . They [the Fifty Days] are not the time of the world which by convention happens to be associated with his resurrection. They are really his time, his day, called into existence by his being made Lord.[17]

The Content of Our Contemplation

The content of our "contemplation" in this book will be the celebrations, whose texts now appear in the *Lectionary* and *Sacramentary,* for the Sundays of Lent, the Days of the Paschal Triduum, and the Sundays of Easter. Regarding the Scripture readings, for two reasons we will consider only those in Series A. First, these particular scripture texts portray the phases of our journey of conversion: purification and enlightenment during Lent, and reflection on the implications of initiation into the Body of Christ during the Easter Time. In fact, we could say that this series of scripture readings has been designed specifically for the processes of the RCIA. Secondly, we have decided to look only at this series, because once we have entered into the Paschal Mystery through contemplating and celebrating the dialogue with God in these texts, we will be able, when it is appropriate, to enter into the other two series.[18]

We include in our study the proper Prefaces of the individual Sundays because they have the particular value of bringing the aspect of the Christ-mystery which is specified in any given celebration into the central proclamation of the praise and thanks: the Eucharistic Prayer. We also include special ritual celebrations such as the

Enrollment of the Elect and the Scrutinies because these intensify the celebration of conversion. Quite naturally we include the rites of Triduum and the initiation sacraments at the Easter Vigil.

Furthermore, we would like to stress that we are not trying to help people discover what lies behind the various scriptural texts of the seasons. Our aim is to "start at the other end," as it were: to begin by being in touch with what is happening within our hearts as persons-in-community. By taking long, loving looks at the Scriptures we try to recognize where the seeds of life in them touch areas in our lives that want to grow. Thus, we try to be sensitive to where the scriptural words call us and to recognize how the present liturgical structures help (or hinder) the growth that the Spirit is nurturing.

We also aim to get in touch—somewhat at least—with the demands of discipleship that flow from the celebration of the mystery of the death and rising of Christ vis-à-vis the demands of the present structures of society. We are not searching for a liturgical spirituality, which for "many people has become ambiguous and confusing, . . . some mysterious and self-contained activity, or a secret which can be broken into by study and some spiritual techniques."[19] We are hoping to enter more completely into the Christian life, which is not just a better or more psychologically adequate human life. It is a *new* life that Paul equates with living in and walking in the Spirit (see Gal. 5:25); and this newness becomes the source of fuller human development.

We have come to *know* that when we are filled with admiration we acknowledge in faith the real presence of the Mystery of Christ in our celebrations. This process of acknowledging God as God in the wonderful deeds we celebrate includes accepting their *consequences* not only in terms of praise and thanks but also in terms of commitment. Thus growth will be taken care of from within; as Paul has it, "God made it (faith) grow" (1 Cor. 3:6 NAB).

On that note we are ready to consider the mystery of being chosen by God.

Notes

1. Although these could hardly be the direct words of Jesus, still they are his inasmuch as they are the early Christian application of Jesus to the circumstances of their lives.
2. The prayers in the *Sacramentary of Verona* are close enough to the period when prayers were improvised that we can surmise that their authors realized the import of what they were saying.
3. This prayer appears as the Opening Prayer for the feast of December 25 in the *Sacramentary of Verona:* Deus, qui in humanae substantiae dignitate [dignitatem] et mirabiliter condidisti et mirabilius reformasti: da quesumus, nobis Iesu Christi filii tui divinitatis esse consortes, qui humanitatis nostrae fieri dignatus est particip. See Cunibert Mohlberg, OSB, *Sacramentarium Veronense* (Rome: Casa Editrice Herder, 1956), p. 157, 1.24-25. English translation mine. Two things can be further noted. First, in Christian Latin the word *mirabiliter* carries overtones of being a faith-insight into an act of compassion on the part of God, an act that causes breath-taking surprise. Secondly, the verb *reformasti* does not mean a return to a former condition of wholeness, but rather a forward movement toward the goal of human beings.
4. *The Sacramentary*, p. 183; excerpted from the English translation of *The Roman Missal* © 1973, International Committee on English in the Liturgy, Inc. (New York: Catholic Book Publishing Co., 1974). All further quotations from this text will be identified as *Sac.* with the page number.
5. See Eduard Schillebeeckx, *Jesus: An Experiment in Christology,* translation of *Jesus, het verhal van een levende* by Hubert Hoskins (New York: Vintage Books, 1981), pp. 379-397 and passim, for a helpful insight into the role forgiveness and conversion play in the resurrection appearances to the apostles.
6. Sebastian Moore, *The Crucified Jesus Is No Stranger* (New York: Seabury, 1977), p. 109.

7. Robert Taft, SJ, "The Liturgical Year," *Worship* 55(1981):2-23, especially 18-23.

8. See *Calendarium Romanum* (Rome: Typis Polyglottis Vaticanis, 1969), #21.

9. Our purpose is to name only a few examples, sufficient to illustrate our point.

10. We cannot stress too emphatically how important it is for us to be actively conscious of the presence of God's Spirit in any act of faith, particularly in a communal expression of faith such as the liturgy. A dynamic is present in the back-and-forth movement of dialogue. This dynamic becomes the symbol of the Holy Spirit in faith-dialogue. Thus, when in technical liturgical language we refer to the epiclesis or the calling upon the Holy Spirit, we are not indicating that the Spirit has been absent. On the contrary, we are recognizing our own need to be open to the energies of the Holy Spirit.

11. See Edward Kilmartin, SJ, "A Modern Approach to the Word of God and The Sacraments of Christ: Perspectives and Principles," in Francis A. Eigo, OSA, ed., *The Sacraments: God's Love and Mercy Actualized* (Villanova, Pa.: University of Villanova Press, 1979) passim and especially 89ff.

12. I encountered this expressive word coined by David Power, OMI, in "The Mystery Which Is Worship," in *The Living Light* 16 (1979):174. It means, of course, "making present."

13. David M. Stanley, SJ, *A Modern Scriptural Approach to the Spiritual Exercises* (St. Louis: The Institute of Jesuit Sources, 1971), p. 285. See also the *Constitution on the Sacred Liturgy*, #5.

14. See Mary Pierre Ellebracht, CPPS, *Remarks: on the Vocabulary of the Ancient Orations in the Missale Romanum* (Nijmegen: Dekker & Van de Vegt, 1963), p. 5, together with the further bibliography given there, for the early meaning of *Church*.

15. E. C. Whitaker, *Documents of the Baptismal Liturgy* (London: S.P.C.K., 1960), has gathered many of the early witnesses of baptismal liturgy into a handy volume. See also Hugh Riley, *Christian Initiation* (Washington, D.C.: Consortium Press, 1974), for an excellent treatment and a valuable bibliography.

16. The numbers attached to quotations from this Rite are the numbers of the sections as they appear in the text. The English translation of this rite has been done by the International Committee on English in the Liturgy, Inc. (Washington, D.C.: Publications Office, United States Catholic Conference, 1974). All quotations (except where noted otherwise) from the Rite found in this book are taken from the above source and will be identified as RCIA with the section number.

17. Patrick Regan, OSB, "Fifty Days and Fiftieth Day," *Worship* 55 (1981):198.

18. The Introduction to the *Lectionary,* © 1969, International Committee on English in the Liturgy, states that since these passages (from Series A) are very important to Christian initiation, they may be used for years B and C, especially when candidates for baptism are present (#13.1). The RCIA (#159) also suggests using Series A if a parish has a catechumenate.

19. Alexander Schmemann, *Of Water and the Spirit* (New York: St. Vladimir's Seminary Press, 1974), p. 107.

2

THE MYSTERY OF BEING CHOSEN

Period of Purification and Enlightenment

There comes a point on any journey when the eagerness to arrive at one's destination becomes very intense. The First Sunday of Lent marks such a moment on our way to God. This day evidences a distinct seriousness about the purpose and destination of the faith journey. The catechumens have been traveling along the first stages of this way—evangelization, first conversion, catechesis, growing attraction—and have experienced developing maturity. They have come to a choice-point and are inwardly prepared to make public their desire to be fully initiated into the Church during the celebration of the Easter Sacraments. During Lent the catechumens' commitment becomes more public, and the community of the faithful become even more fully involved with them on their journey into faith. The mutuality essential to the life of the Body of Christ takes a more definite shape during this time. The faithful who have been traveling the path toward God for some time welcome Lent as a time of renewed commitment to the values and ideals of the Christian life. Involvement with the initiation of new members is part of this renewal for the faithful. The situation is described in the *Constitution on the Sacred Liturgy* as follows:

> The season of Lent has a twofold character; primarily by recalling or preparing for baptism and penance, it disposes the faithful who persevere in

hearing the Word of God and in prayer, to celebrate the Paschal Mystery. (L #109)

It is outside the scope of this work to do a history of the development of Lent.[1] We simply want to state that we enter this season with certain legacies that have come to us from Christian practice. One such legacy is the consistent recurrence of three particular gospel pericopes— the Samaritan woman, the man born blind, and Lazarus. All three deal with the mystery of conversion into Christ, and we shall discuss these pericopes in Chapter 3. A second legacy comes to us from the Church's struggle over the question of reconciliation of penitents.[2] The strenuous public penances the Church imposed on those who sought reentry into full communion give us a sense of the heinousness of sin, particularly of sin committed after baptism. Today our celebration of Ash Wednesday reflects the effect of that penitential legacy. At one time, the distribution of ashes had developed an excessively morbid character. Now, however, it has taken on a fuller gospel sense in the formula, "Repent, and believe the Good News" (Mark 1:15).[3] The formula names conversion as good news, and its call to penitence is a call to grow in our relationship with God. Finally, the forty days of preparing for Easter are a gift. They give us sufficient time in which conversion can penetrate our various mental attitudes and emotional reflexes; they give us a time for yearly renewal.

History bequeaths us a heritage that marks Lent as a season of conversion with a threefold thrust: initiation (of catechumens), reconciliation (of penitents), and renewal (of the faithful). As we celebrate the season's beginning on the First Sunday of Lent, we do so in light of this legacy.

On Becoming the Elect

By reflecting on what happens within us as we move along our faith journey, we recognize that purification and enlightenment go on continually throughout life. We can safely say that the Church, through the RCIA, has not established these particular steps in the conversion process as *a priori* prerequisites for full acceptance into Christ. On the contrary, only over the course of time have Christians come to realize that God's invitation to conversion follows a discernible pattern.[4] At first God's call demands that we relinquish what is blatantly sinful. Later it summons us to leave the comfort of any given stage in our growth and to enter into an unknown area of faith. To be authentic, this pattern is only gradually discovered; it cannot be legislated from the outside.

Each call to new growth, when it is accepted, demands greater purification if we are to clarify our vision. As we see more clearly, we recognize our need to be cleansed from sinful tendencies and acts. Thus the process of growth goes on *always motivated from within*. In recognizing this process we also come to realize that we give delight to our Father. Being the chosen ones or the elect not only indicates that those so designated have made the "election" to receive the sacraments of initiation at the Vigil of Easter; it also expresses that the faith community has issued a call to them and now agrees to support them. But there is even more here. For the *mystery* of being chosen and of being the beloved of God catches up not only those seeking initiation, but also those already initiated (the faithful).

The desire to be *special* is built into our nature. Children long to be precious to their parents, lovers desire to be carried in each other's hearts, and friends seek a special place in each other's affection. In each of these examples, the one chosen needs to *know* that he or she has been selected from a motive of love alone.[5] This natural desire to be chosen becomes the basis for our faith desire to be God's chosen ones.

When we look at the history of salvation, we see that God freely chooses whomever he wishes to be his friend. Scripture accents God's initiative and free choice, not discrimination or favoritism. Thus God chooses Abraham,

Isaac, and Jacob. They are God's friends, and God has a mission for them. The same is true of Moses. Even though Moses emerges as a leader by reason of a combination of circumstances and "chance" happenings, still he comes to recognize these events as signs of the gratuity of God's love for the Israelites. Centuries later, when the author of Deuteronomy reflects on the liberation of his people from Egypt, he again reveals God's free choice: "You are a people sacred to the LORD, your God; he has chosen you from all the nations on the face of the earth to be a people peculiarly his own" (Deut. 7:6 NAB). That is a statement of the identity of Israel. Were some stranger to ask, "*Who* are these people?" they could be accurately identified only as "God's holy people," a designation that does not merely describe the Israelites but "identifies" or "names" them. For Israel to exist is to be God's chosen one, who has a special mission to accomplish. This identification holds true throughout Israel's history.

By the time of the exile (ca. 587 B.C.), we find a new and important dimension in the manner of being God's chosen one: servanthood. The Suffering Servant, about whom Deutero-Isaiah sings,[6] is the outstanding example of this type of God's choosing. The mission of this mysterious personage is to save God's people through suffering. Thus the Suffering Servant points to a new mode of God's creative power. Ultimately the Suffering Servant points to the mission Jesus would accomplish through his death and resurrection.

Finally God sends the Son: "This is my beloved Son. My favor rests on him" (Matt. 3:17 NAB). In these words, pronounced by God at Jesus' baptism and repeated at the transfiguration, the Father "identifies" Jesus in terms of unprecedented intimacy. The experience of Jesus' intimate relationship with the Father creates an entire climate of heart that continues "to grow and to give warm clarity and decisive direction to His life."[7] Jesus' motivation, then, is born within the love bond between himself as beloved Son and his Father. We do not try to mimic Jesus' experiences. However, in contemplation we seek to discover that in and with Jesus we, as Christians or as Christians-to-be, share in the mystery of intimacy with the Father.

It is a profound intuition on the part of the Church that while it celebrates its own purification and enlightenment, it also celebrates the mysteries of Jesus' victory over temptation and of his transfiguration on the First and Second Sundays of Lent. Both events reveal Jesus' identity as beloved Son and his mission as servant. Each scripture passage is an anamnesis of a wonderful deed of God: God's being so intimately bound to us that we are enabled to recognize ourselves as God's beloved sons and daughters. On the First Sunday of Lent, the catechumens respond to this divine offer and "identify" themselves as God's holy people by signing their names in the book of the elect (RCIA #22).

Before we move into a deeper consideration of the First and Second Sundays, it may be helpful to repeat the rationale behind our treatment of only parts of the eucharistic celebrations. We do so because we assume that the scripture texts for Lent have been carefully chosen to reveal the mystery of conversion and growth into Christ. In fact, we believe that they grew out of Christian experience of that mystery.[8]

First Sunday of Lent

The Scriptures of the First Sunday of Lent present a stimulating mosaic of contrasts. First, we find the juxtaposition of Adam and Jesus in the face of temptation, each one's experience told with true artistry. Secondly, the contrasts between the beginnings and endings of these stories engender hope. Finally, the reading from Paul places the two protagonists (Adam and Jesus) side by side in a way that evokes disdain for the one and adulation for the other. Taken together, the texts of this Sunday form a jewel of sacred proclamation. Of itself such artistry opens hearts to hear and readies them to accept the Word. Their harmony of the texts is not contrived but is produced out of life experience and therefore evokes eagerness to respond to the Lord, who is building a new creation.

First Reading: Genesis 2:7-9; 3:1-7

Although the First Reading abbreviates the creation story quite a lot, the powerful movement of the story still stirs us. As the story begins, we encounter the first human being, a masterpiece of God the master craftsman. He is not only fashioned by God; he even lives by the very *breath of God:* "The Lord God . . . blew into his nostrils the breath of life." These powerful words express the integrity both of being and of orientation. The human person lives and moves by the breath of God. The reading's conclusion sharply contrasts with its opening. Adam and Eve are left standing in shame. The fig leaves they sew together—hardly adequate covering—aptly symbolize their helplessness. The sacred text artistically effects a climax on the downbeat. The story moves us both by what it says and by the way it says it.[9]

From the first, we recognize ourselves in this story. Adam and Eve are indeed our first parents. When doubts insinuate themselves into commands that God has set within our beings, we realize our own weakness all too poignantly. Even though we sense and know in faith that the law of God is in our hearts, like Eve and Adam we continue to ask, "Is it really true?" The snake gliding in the grass, hidden entirely or only rarely visible, is an apt symbol for similar doubts that echo in our own ears, in our emotions, and even in our hearts. Whenever pride, avarice, lust, gluttony, envy, anger, or sloth rears its head, we sense the uncanny presence of the evil one trying to enter our lives. When times are hard and passion burns, it sounds so right to question, "Is God in our midst, or not?" "Is the supreme power for us, or against us?" "Is

God perhaps fearful and jealous of us, lest we 'become like gods who know what is good and what is bad'?"

Responsorial Psalm: Psalm 51:3-4, 5-6, 12-13, 14, 17

Since God puts the divine law into our hearts, we cannot violate it with impunity. To be unable to form a commitment to God reveals a spiritual immaturity that engenders a sense of shame and nakedness.[10] In the face of such helplessness we can only call for mercy. Today's Responsorial Psalm articulates that call. The words of Psalm 51—the words of one of God's chosen ones—rise spontaneously to our lips. We call for someone to clothe us in the garment of salvation. "Against you only have I sinned. . . . A clean heart create for me. . . . Give me back the joy of your salvation, . . . and my mouth shall proclaim your praise." We plead for the time and the openness to allow the experience of salvation to filter through our whole being.

Gospel: Matthew 4:1-11

The Gospel not only presents a striking contrast to the story of our first parents; it also proclaims the mystery of the undoing of evil, the mystery inaugurated by these words of good news: "Jesus was led into the desert by the Spirit to be tempted by the devil." How upright and integrated Jesus is as he strides into this conflict! He is filled with wonder at his identity as Son, Servant, and Beloved of the Father. In the depth of his person he thrills at the harmony he shares with all creation and with his Father. His mission is to lead all God's children into that harmony. To allow his mission to permeate all his faculties and to deepen his intimacy with the Father, Jesus needs time alone with God, and so he seeks the solitude of the desert.

After fasting forty days and forty nights, Jesus is hungry. Only then does the tempter approach him, and a mighty conflict between the prince of darkness and the Lord of light ensues. An ancient Latin text dramatically sums up the conflict.

Mors et vita duello, Con-flixere mirando.[11]	Life and death con-tended in matchless duel.

We need time to follow the duel, for its outcome affects our lives and the fate of all creation as well. Our liturgical celebration provides that time, for in it we are more than onlookers; by our participation we actually enter into the mystery of Christ's temptation.

In the story, the tempter seeks to undermine the true nature of Jesus' messianic mission by placing before him insidious suggestions: to sustain his life by changing stones into bread, to inspire faith in others by a spectacular leap from the parapet of the Temple, to use political power to spread the Kingdom. Coming as they do when Jesus is hungry, weakened, and lonely, these suggestions seem the more "valid." However, Jesus has been contemplating his own relation with his Father for forty days. And since he has an inner sensitivity to the power in the Word of God, he is able immediately to quote the Word that dispels the first two temptations. Since he is certain that he lives because of the Father and that he wants to be the kind of Son, Servant, and Beloved that his Father wills, he is also able to discern the fallacy in the tempter's use of Scripture. Finally, the impudent third temptation is completely repugnant to the climate of heart that God has created in Jesus during their forty days of intimate communion. In short, Jesus' expulsion of the evil one clearly shows that he is making his decisions from the depths of the divine power within him.

God's Word invites us to identify ourselves with Jesus in the story of his temptation and to make a choice *for* God and *against* the tempter. If we accept the Word's invitation and make that choice, all our relationships become angels ministering to us for wholeness, rather than satanic forces luring us to disintegration.

Second Reading: Romans 5:12-19

Through effective use of juxtaposition, Paul offers us an opportunity to express our joy over the way God chose to remedy the offense of one human. In the face of God's gracious gift of *the* human, Jesus Christ, the havoc and death that reigned so long is overthrown. Human helplessness—even the corporate human helplessness that has escalated into our time—is essentially inferior to the strength of the "one man, Jesus Christ." When the human community, in the power of the Holy Spirit, fully accepts God's gift, our ability to hold out in the face of temptation will know no limit. That is why we constantly need to recall the truth that God saves us *in* the human community—in the communion we call "church."

In Paul's theology we also glimpse a hint of the paradoxical "happy fault" (as the Exsultet calls it)—the advantageous sin—that we will celebrate at the Easter Vigil. Salvation has begun in the person of Jesus. It will continue within the life of the Church communion until the end of time.

One last observation: The desert experience of Jesus demonstrates a fundamental ambiguity of the Christian experience. To scrutinize our motives, to discern and separate the really good and the necessary from the spurious, is no easy matter. Although Christians experience and complain about temptation, today's Gospel shows us that Jesus himself shared our lot, yet triumphed and granted us a share in his victory. "Conversion, love, faith, salvation or whatever you want to call it, occur in ambiguous 'in-between' situations and not otherwise."[12] Ambiguity is painful; it is frightening; it does not provide neat certainty. Ambiguity tests us. If we long for the transformation, the *utterly new* way of decision-making that Christianity offers, like Jesus, we must allow ourselves to face radical uncertainties and permit the Spirit and the Word to guide us. The testing we experience, then, becomes an opening through which the redeemed motive power can penetrate deeper into our being and activity.

God continually insinuates his transforming Word into our life situation and calls us to cross over into new ways of relating to him. Such moments of truth are never of our own making; rather, the Holy Spirit "sets them up." Our choices at these moments of truth, however, are as important as were the choices Jesus made. We are free to accept or to reject the new life God offers, but when we do accept, God gives the increase.

The Rite of Election

After the homily, the community celebrates the Rite of Election. Those catechumens who are ready to confess with their lips what the Lord has been doing in them approach the Church to seek admission. They are ready in faith to ask for the full transformation that they *know* the Lord has been offering them. Their anticipation of this step is both joyful and unsettling. The step is an in-between time calling them to move across a boundary into a new and deeper sharing in the life of the community. Hence sponsors and godparents accompany them and present them to the larger community. These special persons have been making the community real for the prospective new members. It is their faces that the catechumens have come to know, their hands that they have felt. Because of their more intimate involvement with the catechumens, godparents and sponsors also serve as models to whom the faithful can look to discover the importance of Lent not only for the catechumens but for themselves as well. Regarding the importance of Lent for catechumens and faithful alike, the RCIA states:

> The time of purification and enlightenment or illumination of the catechumens customarily

coincides with Lent; both in its liturgy and in its liturgical catechesis, Lent is a memorial or a preparation for baptism and a time of penance. It renews the community of the faithful together with the catechumens and makes them ready to celebrate the paschal mystery which the sacraments of initiation apply to each individual. (RCIA #21)

For these words to be true not only of sponsors and godparents but of all of us, however, we must realize that the journey into faith is a continual one. Both the baptized members of the community and the catechumens are influenced by the dialogue that follows upon the presentation of the candidates. Its inner dynamism shows that the relationship between the catechumens and the baptized has grown to such maturity that *mutual* commitment is possible.

When the president of the assembly calls the catechumens to the Easter Sacraments, he is signaling a very solemn moment. The call makes public and official what has been happening within them. The following are the criteria for admission of new members: listening to the Word of God proclaimed by the Church, change of behavior, fellowship in the community, and common prayer (RCIA #144).

In response to the express call to the Easter Sacraments, the newly chosen sign their names. This action ritualizes two inner realities. On the one hand, it marks their public affirmation that the Lord has called them through the invitation of the Church. On the other, it is a sign of their trust that the Lord will continue his loving invitation and that the Church will continue its support. For candidates and baptized alike, the call to the Easter Sacraments is a summons *now* within *this* celebration to share in the growth that the Spirit is engendering in the Body of Christ. It is a moment of hope. Coming as it does after the Liturgy of the Word, this call expresses again *today* what Christians have long come to anticipate during this season:

Through our observance of Lent
you correct our faults and raise our minds
   to you,
you help us grow in holiness,
and offer us the reward of everlasting life
through Jesus Christ our Lord.[13]

Sponsors and godparents still have the immediate responsibility to continue to support the chosen ones along the way their election has opened up to them. Ideally, though, the entire community, both elect and faithful, should possess a shared understanding—at least in an initial sort of way—of who they are and what they are about together. The words of Scripture that have been proclaimed, "broken open" in the homily, and celebrated in the rite of dialogue and the signing of names, have called all present to move forward on the journey toward the Easter Sacraments. The elect, their catechists, their sponsors, their godparents, their families, the entire community, and those who have not yet chosen to become full members of the Church, all need to realize that they stand in need of the Father's compassion. The intercessions for the elect voice this shared need: "that once they have become children of the promise, they may, please, by the power of your love arrive at eternal life, which they could never achieve by their own natural power."[14]

Since the Rite of Election celebrates both the recognition and the affirmation of our identity, it serves as a strong incentive to growth. The dismissal of the elect before the celebration of the Eucharist greatly increases the symbolic power of the rite. If the elect remained during the eucharistic celebration, their presence would deny that they are not as yet fully integrated into the community of the faithful. Their dismissal flows from reality, and it properly emphasizes the sacraments as real encounters with God. Furthermore, the Church's promise to be present with them at the time of the scrutinies is considerate and gentle: "You have been chosen by God and have entered with us on the way of Lent. May Christ himself be your way, your truth, and your life, especially during the approaching scrutinies when we shall meet with you again. For the present, go in peace." (RCIA #150)

Preface of the First Sunday of Lent

The message proclaimed in the Word, once it has been acknowledged in the Rite of Election, is memorialized further amid praise and thanksgiving to the Father in the Preface proper for this Sunday. In this Preface we find affirmation of Jesus' "fast of forty days [which] makes this a holy season of self-denial" (*Sac.*, p. 397). Mentioning the Lord's victory over the devil, we acknowledge that the Lord is also enabling us to search our motives and to rid ourselves of the hidden corruption of evil. Finally, the Preface proclaims the goal of the entire process of proclamation, acknowledgment, and praise: that by sharing in the paschal meal we may celebrate "its fulfillment in the promised land of heaven" (*Sac.*, p. 397). All of this is actualized within our celebration today. The special anamnesis of the Preface colors the entire Eucharistic Prayer, and our sharing in the sacred meal brings us the food and drink that is beyond being "bread alone" and that strengthens the Church in its mission of continuing to build the Kingdom of God.

In conclusion, on the First Sunday of Lent we celebrate Christ, the new Adam; we celebrate both his first step on the way to his Easter passage and our journey with him. Our season of conversion and renewal—our desert experience—has begun. We, elect and faithful alike, are now embroiled in a conflict with the powers of evil. In the desert called Lent, God summons us to take the time to discover who and whose we are (i.e., to contemplate), to deepen our intimacy with God, and to ready ourselves to celebrate the joy of Christ's Easter passage. The Prayer for the Elect that we offer during today's Rite of Election says it all.

Today we begin Lent and look forward to our celebration of the life-giving mysteries of our Lord's suffering, death, and resurrection. These chosen men (and women), whom we lead with us to the Easter sacraments, look to us for an example of Christian life. Let us pray to the Lord for them and for ourselves that we may be strengthened by each other's mutual efforts, and so come to share the joys of Easter. (RCIA #148)

Second Sunday of Lent

As we approach the Second Sunday of Lent, we must recall that what is proclaimed in the Liturgy of the Word in story, in song, in exhortation, and in prayer becomes an event today for us who celebrate. This means that today we preview the full celebration of the Paschal Mystery; we learn what it will entail for us in terms of total giving; and we glimpse the glory that will follow. In other words, *we* are the ones transfigured in Christ to become, in him, Son, Beloved, Servant. The sacred liturgy today is manifestly a celebration of our being God's elect, chosen ones of God. All this takes place by the power of the Holy Spirit. Thus our identification with Christ is *real*, even as the power to live this identification is real. We begin our examination of this Sunday by looking to its main reading, the Gospel.

Gospel: Matthew 17:1-9

What does our identification with Jesus mean in terms of his transfiguration? We, the entire assembly, are chosen to ascend the Mount of Tabor with Jesus. In our celebration Jesus' personal intimacy with the Father is revealed to us, and the Lord calls us to share that intimacy. Almost in the same breath, God's Word introduces us to the mystery of the death and resurrection of Christ. Each gospel account of the transfiguration includes the mention of the passover of Jesus. It is part of the injunction laid on the apostles on the way down from the mountain: "Do not tell anyone of the vision until the Son of Man rises from the dead." Thus by anticipation the Word already inserts us into the dying and rising of Jesus, and we hold ourselves ready to enter into the full celebration of the Paschal Mystery during the Sacred Triduum.

Several other details of the Gospel demand our attention. God deals with his people in ways that are ever ancient and ever new. God always shapes encounters with us according to what we already know. We are not surprised, then, that today's story is told in terms that carry significant overtones for us as well as for the three apostles. We find Jesus ascending the mountain to receive for himself, and for us with him, further affirmation of intimacy with the Father. From this intimacy, as we have seen,[15] our mission flows. Jesus is the new Moses who meets God on the mountain and there receives further insight into *how* he will become the one mediator of the New Covenant.

This covenant is personal. Jesus is not untouchable, as was Sinai, destined to cast fear and trembling into the people (Heb. 12:18-24). On the contrary, Jesus in his very person is the acme, the culmination, of human contact with God. As such, he brings God into our immediate human situation. Jesus is at once the unique tabernacle (tent) where God dwells, and the fullest expression of personal encounter with God. And these two—tent and encounter—are one! The face of Moses was radiant after he had met God atop Mount Sinai; the entire person of Jesus and even his garments shine with transcendent glory in the transfiguration.

Moses and Elijah[16] represent the entire Law and Prophets. Each, in turn, is now being fulfilled in Christ Jesus. They signal to us that the Word of God is never comprehended in its entirety. Often it is sensed only dimly for a long time. Then, through purification and further enlightenment, a kind of "fullness of time" arrives for us, even as it did for Peter. Peter is not mistaken when he says, "Lord, how good it is for us to be here!" He senses, however vaguely, that the transfiguration represents his heart's desire. He longs to provide tents of encounter. He is shortsighted in that he wants to settle in too soon. Peter does not as yet realize that Jesus has to die to enter into his glory. Like Peter, we learn this only gradually. In fact, our hesitation also resembles that of Jesus who struggled with the awful specter of Calvary when he faced it in the Garden of Olives.

The cloud from which God's voice emanates links the transfiguration to other theophanies.[17] It appropriately symbolizes the mystery at hand, for it both reveals the active presence of God in the human heart and conceals it. On Tabor, as on Sinai, the voice from the cloud confirms the vision: "This is my beloved Son, on whom my favor rests. Listen to him." To listen to Jesus is actually to listen to the Word of God made flesh and to see his glory (John 1:14). When we celebrate God's Word, therefore, we already live in the power of the resurrection.

First Reading: Genesis 12:1-4

The First Reading for this Sunday proclaims God's call to Abram. This call to faith in the one God is coupled with a promise: "I will make of you a great nation. . . ." A promise belongs to the language of love. It engages both the power and the fidelity of the lover—in this case, God. Two facets of Abram's call indicate an implicit promise. First of all, the call involves Abram and engages his heart. It genuinely inclines him to follow. The call seems to touch something within him that is already struggling to emerge. Abram has a sense of "Yes, I want this," much as lovers do when they begin to sense commitment growing within their hearts. Secondly, the call does not include any definite material boundaries: "Go . . . to a land that I will show you." Only *after* he goes does Abram discover the perimeters of the land to which he is called, and even then the call's implications remain vague.

This reading reveals both that God's call and his promise to Abram are *ours* as well and that they combine to form an inner drive of faith in our lives. Indeed, when we are sensitive to what the Lord is accomplishing in us as a people by the power of the Holy Spirit, then—whether consciously or subliminally—we find God's words to Abram stirring within us—"burning," the disciples at Emmaus call it (Luke 24:32). Every call from the Lord is a call to cross from where we are at any given moment and to venture into the unknown. The territory to which God calls us is never familiar, but always one that God *will* show us. Moreover, everything conducive to growth will be a blessing, and what is inimical to growth will be a curse. We do not have to reflect long to recognize how true this is. We may experience painful confusion, doubt, and even sins as we struggle to answer the call of God. But these need not hinder our growth—at least not permanently—as long as we struggle in the depths of our being to say yes.

The last part of God's promise continues today: "All the communities of the earth shall find blessing in you." We desperately need to count on the universality of that promise. It is difficult for many to recognize how the communities of the earth are finding a blessing in their associations with descendants of Abraham. As nations and as individuals we are radically in need of conversion, of a new way of relating to others. If, like Abraham, we wish to go as the *Lord* directs, we can no longer wage war against other nations nor exploit them financially.

There is still another area where this word from Genesis needs to be a two-edged sword. The faith of Abraham, which has been fulfilled in Christ, is meant to be a blessing to all peoples, all cultures. Thus the good news, since it is always in the form of our believing answer to God's word, must really be enfleshed in our own culture. We need discernment in this area on two accounts. First of all, we can mistake a cultural attitude as faith. Like Peter on Tabor, we can refuse to accept a suffering Messiah; or again, we can insist that our cultural practices are essential for salvation and try to impose them on others.[18] God told Abraham to *leave* his culture—his country and his father's house. Secondly, the heart and center of faith always needs to be the motivating force behind our response to God's call: "Go . . . to a land that I will show you." If we adhere firmly to a personal relationship with God, we will be able to incarnate that faith in *any* culture without getting lost in false or deceptive values of that culture. If we wish to maintain such personal relationship with God in the technological world—which is a foreign land to many of us—we will perforce be called to a deeper conversion. We will finally plant the message of God and enlist even technology in the service of the Kingdom. Thus the Word of God calls us through Abraham to a thoroughgoing purification and enlightenment in order to discover how we can incarnate God's Word in our work, in our homes, in our own culture, and in all cultures.

Responsorial Psalm: Psalm 33:4-5, 18-19, 20, 22

The message of the First Reading—our need to respond unreservedly to God's call—makes us realize how much we need the Lord. The cantor places on our lips a most appropriate refrain in the response to the First Reading: "Lord, let your mercy be on us, as we place our trust in you." This refrain, together with other verses from Psalm 33, signifies our complete trust in the Lord.

Second Reading: 2 Timothy 1:8-10

In the Second Reading Paul proclaims the result of his reflection on God's merciful dealings with his people. "The grace held out to us in Christ Jesus before the world began . . . [is] now made manifest through the appearance of our Savior." Paul immerses us into the plan of God again, the plan that Lent mirrors so well. God robbed death of its power (purification). God brought life and immortality into clear light (enlightenment). We need only look into Paul's words, and lovingly look again, to recognize their truth for us.

Preface of the Second Sunday of Lent

In the Preface for this Sunday we again make memorial of the close and necessary relationship between death and resurrection: " . . . the promised Christ had first to suffer and so come to the glory of his resurrection." This anamnesis clearly identifies (names) the meaning of the transfiguration. It also states, in so many words, what we often take for granted in each eucharistic celebration: that the supreme gift of Christ in the crucifixion is made present to us and for us so that we may live the glorified life. To the extent that Christ is Lord, that is, to the extent he is the motivation for all we do, our lives are already transfigured (transcendent).

The environment in which these words are proclaimed shapes their fecundity in much the same way that the condition of the soil affects the productivity of the seeds planted in it. Thus on the Second Sunday of Lent the power of the Word of the Lord depends on how eagerly the community is looking toward its Easter passage and on how closely its members are bonded in forgiveness and love.

In short, on the first two Sundays of Lent we celebrate our identity with Christ the beloved of the Father. We have undertaken to journey toward fuller sharing in this prerogative. This realization that we are fully accepted by God is of paramount importance. "A person can only confess to his fault when he is certain of receiving forgiveness."[19] Such certainty is a faith reality that has to be experienced; it can never be contrived. Patience is of the essence, for we find ourselves seesawing between "already" and "not yet." Certain of God's acceptance, we have already been able to confess our sins. Still, we know that we are people on the way and that our transfiguration is a gradual process. In other words, although we know a "touch of glory," still we enter into "gory" moments as well—moments when we feel so unworthy that we are tempted to doubt God's unconditional love.

To say then that we have been again called out of the darkness of sin into the fuller light of victory over the evil one and that we are already basking in the glory of the transfigured Lord is a figurative way of expressing our assurance that we have been fully accepted by God through Jesus. We look forward to celebrating this acceptance in the Paschal Sacraments when "we, with our unveiled faces reflecting like mirrors the brightness of the Lord, all grow brighter and brighter as we are turned into the image that we reflect; this is the work of the Lord who is Spirit" (2 Cor. 3:18 JB).

Notes

1. A number of sources describe the history of Lent: A. G. Martimort, *L'Eglise en Prière: Introduction à la Liturgie* (Paris: Desclée, 1961), pp. 214-232 and 693-723. See W. J. O'Shea, "Lent," *New Catholic Encyclopedia* (St. Louis, Mo.: McGraw-Hill Publishing Co., 1967) 8:634-636, with bibliography.
2. For a description of the Rites of Public Penance, see J. A. Jungmann, SJ, *Die lateinischen Bussriten in ihrer geschichtliche Entwicklung* (Innsbruck: Rauch, 1932). See also P. F. Palmer, "Penance, The Sacrament of," in *New Catholic Encyclopedia*, ibid., 5:73-78. See also the excellent series *The Rite of Penance: Commentaries:* vol. 1: Ralph Keifer and Frederick R. McManus, eds., *Understanding the Document;* vol. 2: Elizabeth McMahon Jeep, ed., *Implementing the Rite;* vol. 3, Nathan Mitchel, OSB, ed., *Background and Directions* (Washington, D.C.: The Liturgical Conference, 1978). The last-named volume includes an article by Nathan Mitchel, "The Many Ways to Reconciliation: An Historical Synopsis of Christian Penance," which gives an insightful description of how the Rite of Public Penance was modeled after the Initiation Process. See pp. 27-32 especially.

3. *The Jerusalem Bible* (Garden City, N.Y.: Doubleday & Company, Inc., 1966). All further quotations taken from this translation will be identified with the letters JB.

4. Modern works on spirituality also bear witness to this conversion "pattern." Herbert Smith, SJ, *The Pilgrim Contemplative*, vols. 1 and 2 (Collegeville, Minn.: Liturgical Press, 1977), pp. 9-14. Furthermore, certain aspects of the mystery of conversion and growth in the life of union with God seem to arise in similar forms. Thus for a long time the designation of these stages of conversation was (a) the purgative way, (b) the illuminative way, (c) the unitive way. This terminology seems to be reflected in the RCIA's designation of the period of Lent as the Period of Purification and Enlightenment.

5. See Conrad W. Baars, *Born Only Once: The Miracle of Affirmation* (Chicago: St. Anthony Messenger Press, 1975). This interesting book gives many insights into the need for affirmation and the need to be someone's chosen one.

6. There are four Suffering Servant songs: Isa. 42:1-4; 49:1-7; 50:4-11; 52:13-53:12.

7. G. A. Aschenbrenner, SJ, "Hidden in Jesus before the Father," *Review for Religious* 34 (1975):127.

8. All scriptural quotations found in this work's treatment of the Sundays of Lent, of Triduum, and of the Sundays and feasts of Easter Time are taken directly from the English translation of the *Lectionary for Mass,* © 1970, Confraternity of Christian Doctrine, Washington, D.C., and from *The Roman Missal,* © 1970, Confraternity of Christian Doctrine, Washington, D.C.; English translations of the antiphons, © 1969, International Committee on English in the Liturgy, Washington, D.C. Since the scriptural quotations are taken *directly* from the *Lectionary's* translation of the Scripture for the particular feast, they do not bear specific chapter and verse references except where deemed necessary, and except for section headings. The author of this work presumes that the reader will utilize the *Lectionary* as a reference as he or she reads this text.

9. Recently, much has been written to reinstate story as a legitimate form of catechesis. This has happened because we have discovered that life is marked by a series of crisis moments. To pass through them, we need to recognize

the movement within each crisis: its beginning, its middle or adventure, and its end. Story serves as a guide through crisis by inviting the listener to enter into the protagonist's crisis, to experience its movements with the protagonist, and finally, to be thrilled by the ending. Some current references on story include: Mark Searle, "The Journey of Conversion," *Worship* 54 (January, 1980):35-55; John Shea, *Stories of God: An Unauthorized Biography* (Chicago: The Thomas More Press, 1978), and *Stories of Faith* (Chicago: The Thomas More Press, 1980); and Robert Bela Wilhelm, *Storytelling for Self-Discovery* (Kansas City, Mo.: NCR Cassettes).

10. We may try to hide our shame, we may use various gimmicks—such as psychological facades—or we may try to run away from the truth, but we can never be any more successful than Adam and Eve were. We know a depth of helplessness that we fear to admit and that we are unable to plumb by our human power, even though all the while we do somehow realize deep down that non-admission is devastating.

11. The verses quoted in Latin are part of the Sequence for Easter Sunday.

12. Rosemary Haughton, *The Transformation of Man* (London: Templegate, 1967), p. 271.

13. Lenten Preface IV (Weekdays), *Sacramentary*, p. 395.

14. *Ordo Initiationis Christianae Adultorum* (OICA) #149 (my translation).

15. See pp. 30-31.

16. Elijah met God on Mount Horeb (1 Kings 19:8-18).

17. Human beings become aware of God's presence and commands in ways that are at once clear and unclear; a voice from a cloud becomes an excellent metaphor to express such revelation. Scriptural examples of this abound: e.g., in Exodus 3:4-10 Moses "saw" and "heard" God in the voice from the burning bush, where God's identity and Moses' mission came together; in Exodus 19:9-25 God spoke from the cloud, lightning, and smoke on Sinai to give the ten commandments as terms of the covenant; Isaiah 6:1-13 recounts Isaiah the prophet's experience of God as the All-holy and of his mission to be God's spokesman; Psalm 29:3-9 sings of God's voice revealed in wind and thunder and of God's countenance in the lightning

while those who recognize these signs say "Glory!" In the New Testament (Matt. 3:16-17 and the parallel passages in Luke and Mark), God's voice was heard from the cloud at the baptism of Jesus revealing Jesus' identity and mission; the transfiguration (Matt. 17:1-8) again offers the voice from the cloud revealing Jesus as Son and also as the one whose mission it was to save the world by his passage from death to new life; Acts 1:7-11 reveals Jesus, after he gave the apostles their mission, being received into the cloud, the divine presence; Acts 2:1-12 reveals this same presence in the reverse order: First, there is the sound of the driving wind, then the appearance of the fiery tongues that sat on each of the apostles, whose bold proclamations became the voice of God's revelation. The anonymous mystic who describes his experiences of God as *The Cloud of Unknowing,* in the manuscript dating from the fourteenth century, is right in line with the long history of God's merciful self-revelation. An excellent edition of this work has been published by Ira Progoff (New York: Dell Publishing Company, 1956).

18. See Vincent J. Donovan, *Christianity Rediscovered* (Notre Dame: Fides/Claretian, 1978) for excellent insights into the confusion between culture and faith.

19. Sebastian Moore, op. cit., p. 99.

3

THE MYSTERY OF THE STRUGGLE FOR ENTRY INTO NEW LIFE

The selections from the Gospel of John read on the Third, Fourth, and Fifth Sundays of Lent proclaim the essential process of conversion that leads to initiation into the Church. This chapter attempts to show both how the Church celebrates this mystery today and how today's Church views the process of conversion.

God always respects human freedom. God approaches us not by imposing commands but by encountering us in dialogue. Because we cannot know the mind of God before we surrender to God's workings within us, and because God allows the human partner in the dialogue to exercise freedom, we never know ahead of time how the dialogue will turn out. In other words, the dialogue is *real, now,* and never predetermined.

There is both an inner and an outer dialogue, and God is involved in both. The former takes place when the Spirit causes a certain uneasiness, dissatisfaction, or thirst within the heart of an individual or a people which, in turn, creates an outer dialogue, a readiness to accept further divine invitations. Put in another way, our uneasiness is an indication that something new is striving to come to life. When the living Word proclaimed in the assembly touches this germ of newness, growth happens, and we can cross another boundary on our journey to God. For the person thus readied by the action of the Holy Spirit, the passages from Scripture actually "startle, deepen, and reconfigure faith."[1]

Obviously, there is some commonality in the rich variety of God's dealings with humankind, as the Gospels show. The passages from John's Gospel, which the Church proclaims in Cycle A on the Third, Fourth, and Fifth Sundays of Lent—and allows, even prefers, for any Cycle—reveal successive breakthroughs along the way of conversion. They express a universally human and ongoing experience. Coming at this point in our annual celebration of the Easter passage, they have great liturgical significance.

We can readily see why the three gospel pericopes mentioned above have maintained themselves over the ages. When Lent lasted only three weeks, these were the three Sunday gospel texts.[2] They do delineate the shape of conversion to Christ remarkably well. In our day, though, we desire to celebrate the mystery of the Passion of Christ as the source and summit of all Christian struggle. Hence Passion (Palm) Sunday gathers into itself the entire journey we have traveled thus far, and it opens the door to the climax of it all, the Sacred Triduum.

We will now look more closely at the celebrations of the Third, Fourth, Fifth, and Sixth Sundays of Lent so that we may be moved to more complete commitment.

Third Sunday of Lent:
Dialogue Becomes an Inner Dynamic

Gospel: John 4:5-42

Today's gospel story is an outstanding example of the primacy of the relational, both in conversion and in growth in holiness. The back-and-forth of dialogue brings persons into one another's presence, carries them beyond their separateness as individuals, and produces a dynamism by which they influence one another from within.

It is certainly no accident that the scene of the gospel story is Jacob's well. This well had a long and important history in Israel. For centuries it was the source of fresh and clear spring water ("living water"), and many important events took place beside it. To hear that its waters were deep and inaccessible touches a sensitive chord in the human heart, whose vitality also lies deep below the surface of mere appearances. Its depth symbolizes the new life given by Christ.

The well's depth also symbolizes our tendency to hold on to layers of protective covering in order to shield ourselves from the hurt and shame that disclosure might entail. All the while, the buried vitality causes another pain as it struggles to emerge. It usually takes another person, one who is both sensitive and compassionate, to facilitate our descent into the dark passages of the well to discover our true self.

The Samaritan woman is fortunate indeed that such a person meets her. As she faces Jesus of Nazareth across the open well, she has good reason to expect him to despise her, for he is male and a Jew, while she is a woman and a member of a despised people. The moment is tense and, it would seem, impossible for producing anything good. Yet Jesus brings about a healing relationship by proclaiming "good news" to her.

The story also becomes "good news" for us in our liturgical celebration. As a story it has universal appeal. Both the elect and the baptized can "move around" in it. We can all meet Christ at our own well, for we all have unexplored depths wherein lie hidden failures but also hidden possibilities. If we allow him, Jesus will enable us to move further into those depths, and there find more fully the one who is himself the living water.

We can distinguish several levels in Jesus' dialogue with the woman which parallel the steps the Father traveled in saving the entire human family. In Jesus the Son, the Father finally reveals himself. Jesus demonstrated his solidarity with us by taking "the form of a slave, being born in the likeness of men" (Phil. 2:7 NAB). He did not cling to his divinity as he sojourned among us.[3] In this way he assured us of his presence. He first took the time to listen to fearful human beings and to unveil to them a different set of values. For we human beings are often like the Samaritan woman: We do not immediately recognize the surge deep within calling us to a new and entirely different system of values. Then Jesus was able to reveal himself personally as the incarnate compassion of the Father, as the Messiah sent to redeem us.

Jesus moves through this same process with the Samaritan woman. Tired and thirsty from his journey, Jesus identifies himself with the woman, who is also tired and thirsty. She is tired from her many trips to the well. But beyond physical weariness, she also knows a boredom at the core of her being, and no water from Jacob's well can relieve that tedium! When Jesus asks her for a drink, he expresses his own neediness and identifies with the woman in her thirst. At that moment Jesus' thirst becomes the symbol of his desire to be Messiah to the woman. It initiates the healing that will take place through the ensuing dialogue.

When the woman refuses to respond to him (of herself she cannot do so), Jesus sets aside his own thirst and his eagerness for a simple human response. He listens obediently to her; he sojourns with her, absorbing her rebuffs (John 4:8-9, 11-12). Jesus dares to stand by her and to believe in her. He remains strongly personal and thereby touches her in a way that transforms her fears into new and positive experiences.

Gradually Jesus enables the woman to move beyond vain self-reliance and to request living water from him. Once she is in contact with him, Jesus reveals her deep desire to be rid of her sins. Now truth breaks forth, and the woman admits that Jesus is a prophet. This admission leads her (and us with her) right into the arms, as it were, of Jesus as Messiah. His full self-revelation sends the woman off into the town to spread the "good news," to evangelize.

What a masterpiece of dialogue this is! Its inner dynamism is easily discernible, even palpable. It involves the whole human person: body, psyche, and spirit. The well is the source of water indispensable for human life on the physical level. The dialogue becomes the arena where the initial relationship with Jesus occurs. Jesus understands himself to be the living water. He is able to plumb the depths of the Samaritan woman's heart and, through his understanding dialogue with her, reveals himself as the one who gives life. The well, then, becomes a metaphor of Jesus as Lord and Christ, and specifically a metaphor of the baptismal encounter with Christ. "No one can enter into God's kingdom without being begotten of water and Spirit" (John 3:5 NAB).

Something remains to be said about the artistic form of this Johannine dialogue that depicts the struggle of a person endeavoring to rise from the things of this world to belief in Jesus.[4] The dialogue seems to be contrived. Not only does Jesus engage the woman on the topic of water to quench his thirst, but his words seem to be purposely enigmatic, designed to produce the very objections that will give the scriptural author the opportunity to place words of a predetermined revelation on the lips of Jesus. There can be little doubt that the author is using this stylized form of dialogue to serve his own theological reflection. We, the celebrating community, find that this artistic form of dialogue stimulates our own thirst for "living water," which we recognize as Jesus' own revelation of himself in his gift of the Spirit.[5] "It was in one Spirit that all of us . . . were baptized into one body. All of us have been given to drink of the one Spirit" (1 Cor. 12:13 NAB). Gradually we identify with the new revelations that come to us in the dialogue. We acknowledge the unique challenge that Jesus is offering today—in our midst—to both the elect and the faithful on our journey to the Paschal Sacraments. We long to have that same water spring up to eternal life within us and to be able to worship in spirit and in truth. We also catch a first, faint aroma of the food that will sustain our new life. When the apostles return with food, Jesus introduces us to the truth that he lives by the will of his Father, which is for us a metaphor of the real meaning of Eucharist. Finally, because commitment to Christ is the source of our mission, the dialogue also raises the metaphor of the harvest. By returning to her village and spreading the good news of her conversion to Christ, the Samaritan woman becomes an apostle.

This Gospel finds "flesh" today through the presence of the catechumens among us. It speaks tellingly of their coming to faith, for it relates the faith journey not only of one Samaritan woman but of all who travel the path of Christ's Easter passage. Through his Spirit-filled Word, the Lord invites seekers to faith (John 4:10). In dialogue and the sharing of story, fledgling faith matures, and God quenches our thirst for meaning with the revelation that Jesus is the Messiah. Today this revelation happens through the ministry of the supporting, witnessing community of faith—those who make the faith journey with the catechumens. After the catechumens celebrate the Easter Sacraments, they will be able to share their faith with others, to spread the good news (RCIA #19), and to say to us, the faithful, "No longer does our faith depend on your story. We have heard for ourselves, and we know that this really is the Savior of the world" (John 4:42).

First Reading: Exodus 17:3-7

The First Reading is a masterpiece of simplicity. It relates the primitive story of how the thirsty Israelites rebelled against God in the desert and how God responded by ordering Moses to strike the rock with his staff. As in today's Gospel, thirst for water serves as a symbol of human longing for a relationship with God. The Israelites' ungrateful grumbling, "Is the Lord in our midst or not?" does not belie their thirst for God; in fact, it highlights it. Their murmuring is no half-hearted human act. The people are angry and rebellious because they do not trust God's power and concern. Even Moses almost loses heart, and he cries out to God in fear. Like a human father, God knows how to deal with a stubborn son.[6] God does not argue, cajole, browbeat, scold, or threaten. God simply astounds the people with a surprise that takes their breath away. No need to search for a logical sequence between the people's behavior and God's subsequent action; there is none. There is only the free choice of a Father who is wildly prodigal in his love. Such love has a pacifying effect on the people and enables them to accept God in faith.

We do not have to explain or draw a moral from this story. The message explodes before us and within us. Contemplation helps us identify with the Israelites' situation and recognize in ourselves the hardness of the rock. There, in the deepest recesses of our heart, we come to *know* the divine power when God brings living water from its depths.[7] The story itself is a *vital* symbol: It effects its own application particularly within the liturgical celebration.

Instinctively we notice in ourselves an inner movement toward God. Psychologists never tire of pointing out how a father's unconditional love has this effect on his children. When in faith we recognize that our hard hearts desire to become loving, we know that God is accomplishing a deed even greater than bringing forth water from rock. God is bringing forth love from hearts of stone. God is also extending an invitation to decision, a decision that flows—oddly enough—from our very hardness in sin. On this Sunday, then, we catch another glimpse of the mystery of the *felix culpa*—happy fault—that we will proclaim at the Easter Vigil.

Responsorial Psalm: Psalm 95:1-2, 6-7, 8-9

In summary, today's First Reading provides a loving look at the wonderful way God deals with his rebellious children. God's way of purifying the sinner is not to punish, but to overwhelm him or her with concern and power. Our liturgical celebration, therefore, bursts forth in recognition of God's powerful concern for us: "If *today* you hear his voice, harden not your hearts!" (Emphasis mine.)

The psalm plays on the words *hard hearts* and evokes streams of memories about the way the Lord loves us *as we are.* In our response to the Word we recognize that God uses our sins and infidelities—our hardness of heart—to encounter us and to overwhelm us with love. Amid the rocks and the hot, dry sand of the desert, we can dance with glee as we acclaim the Rock of our salvation, for "he is our God, and we are the people he shepherds."

Second Reading: Romans 5:1-2, 5-8

This reading is a theological reflection on the process revealed in the First and Third Readings. It proclaims that our hope will not be disappointed, because the Holy Spirit has been given to us. Who better than the elect can realize that "when we were still powerless Christ died for us"? The Word also renews the entire assembly, for it is proclaimed to a people on the march, a people who make their Easter passage together.

Our celebration, begun in Word and Response, takes on an even more definitive form in the Scrutiny celebrated today with the elect.

First Scrutiny

The three Scrutinies found in the RCIA evolved from ancient Christian practice.[8] They celebrate successive stages of conversion, our spiritual journey. Enlightened by a deeper knowledge of Christ, the elect can now examine their minds and hearts more closely. The Scrutiny Rite is the celebration of God's twofold action: of healing whatever the elect have discerned as weak, defective, or sinful in themselves, and of strengthening whatever is upright, strong, and holy in them (see RCIA #25.1, #154, #156, #157). Since the three Scrutinies are intimately bound to the rest of the liturgical celebration on the Third, Fourth, and Fifth Sundays of Lent respectively, we will consider only the first one here and will discuss the other two in their proper places.

The Rite itself begins with a kind of informal introductory movement when the elect and their godparents/sponsors come before the presider, who then invites the entire congregation to pray for the elect. While the elect either stand with head bowed or kneel in prayer, the godparents/sponsors express their personal support by laying a hand on the shoulder of the one they are sponsoring, continuing this gesture while the faithful pray the litany for the elect: that they interiorize the Word of God, learn to know Christ as Savior, acknowledge their sins, and reject what displeases Christ, and that the Holy Spirit strengthen their weakness and teach them to know God.

After the litany the Scrutiny Rite moves into its most important element, the exorcism, which consists of two parts—prayer and the laying on of hands (RCIA #164). Even a cursory glance at the prayers will reveal that this exorcism is the direct opposite of the caricatures we see in the movies. The first part of the prayer capsulizes the message of the Gospel and breaks open its meaning.[9] In this prayer, we praise the Father for having sent the Son, we present the elect to God and ask God to deliver them from the power of the evil one. When we respond "Amen," we are expressing our agreement with, and our entry into, *all of these movements* through Christ our Lord.

Gestures play a significant role in this part of the Rite. First, the presider lays hands on the heads of the elect individually and in silence. This is a gesture of the Father's acceptance. Then the presider extends his hands in a protective gesture over the heads of the entire group and prays that Jesus will break the power of Satan in these chosen ones and will protect them from further attacks.

The second part of the exorcism is a prayer addressed to Christ under a variety of titles. It requests several healings for the elect. The heart of the exorcism asks, in the power of the name of Jesus, that Christ himself be present and save: "Take command of the evil spirit whom you conquered by your rising from the dead. In the Holy Spirit show your chosen ones the way, that as they approach the Father they may adore him in truth."[10] In our concern for the elect we call upon Jesus to conquer their enemy and our enemy as well.

> Here we are not operating on the level of theological reflection, one step removed from the immediacy of Christian experience. Rather there is a vitality and freshness that renders the prayer a living experience of the Lord's power.[11]

With the dismissal of the elect the Scrutiny ends. The faithful enter into the celebration of the Eucharist proper and bring into it what the Lord has accomplished in them through his action on behalf of the elect.

Preface of the Third Sunday of Lent

The Preface expresses the reality that we remember and thus make present.

> When he asked the woman of Samaria for water to drink,
> Christ had already prepared for her the gift of faith.
> In his thirst to receive her faith
> he awakened in her heart the fire of your love.
>
> (*Sac.*, p. 401)

The Preface demonstrates how Jesus always initiates relationship with himself. Jesus' natural thirst for water symbolizes his inner thirst for relationship with the woman. Alluding to today's First Reading, the Preface also speaks of Christ's awakening love in "hard hearts." The Preface's proclamation of this wonderful deed is the good news of the Gospel in "concentrated" form. In turn, this initial stage in the mystery of conversion becomes part of, and is inserted into, our celebration of the total impact that Jesus has on us in his Paschal

Mystery as we express it in the Eucharistic Prayer—
particularly in the Narrative of the Institution.

Fourth Sunday of Lent: Obstacles Become Power

Conversion, if it is authentic, is ongoing, becoming more
deep-rooted and all-pervasive in our lives. Through the
words of Sacred Scripture proclaimed in the assembly,
God calls us ever onward.[12] During the season of Lent,
when we are contemplating and celebrating with special
emphasis our journey into faith, we have to be on guard
against over-systematizing this life process. The deeply
intuitive character of Scripture, particularly of the Gospels, cannot be narrowed into fixed categories without
losing something vital. Because the action of the Holy
Spirit in the Word touches the particular area where the
Holy Spirit is working within the hearts of the faithful,
the Word of God is something new each time it is proclaimed. Liturgical celebration—of the Scrutinies, and
even more, of the Eucharist—always needs to be a sensitive response to the Spirit's vital activity. Conversion
happens when *God* gives the increase in God's own times
and seasons. In a liturgical celebration, word and sacrament together symbolize both this action of God and
our growth in loving response to God. Together they
constitute a continuing dialogue.

Gospel: John 9:1-41

In today's Gospel, Jesus, the eternal light of the world,
anoints the blind man's eyes with mud-paste made with
the Savior's own saliva. Jesus then sends the man off to
bathe in the pool of Siloam. When the man returns, able
to see, we sense the presence of the sacrament of baptism
in germinal form. Both we and the catechumens grow
in our conviction of what the Paschal Sacraments hold
out to us. This conviction, in turn, provides us inner
power to continue the journey to the full encounter with
the Son of Man during the great Vigil.

Even a cursory glance at the Gospel discloses how circumstances subsequent to the blind man's having received his sight bring about new challenges in the conversion process. First, the change in his social status—he is a blind beggar no longer—brings him into various conflicts that call him to further openness in his search for God's meaning in each encounter: with curious neighbors, fearful parents, and unbelieving rulers of the synagogue. Each episode in the story leads him to a boundary situation or a choice-point that he has to pass successfully before approaching fuller acceptance of Christ. We, the celebrating community, find ourselves somewhere in these stages of acceptance.

At this point we will explore the several boundaries that the man passes over as he moves along the way to faith. Jesus initiates the entire process by smearing spittle-mud on the man's eyes and telling him to wash in Siloam.[13] From the moment when the man receives his sight, the movement toward full faith keeps on accelerating each time he encounters opposition. The idle curiosity of friends and neighbors mediates his movement to the first boundary. It is futile for them to ask, "Where is he [Jesus]?" because the once-blind man has never *seen* Jesus. Yet we catch our breath when we hear him say, "I have no idea," for he has washed in the pool at the command of the One *sent* to be the light of the world. We are not disappointed, however, at his answer at the second boundary; for when the Pharisees accost him with "Since it was your eyes he opened, what do you have to say about him?" we hear the man respond, "He is a prophet." No one can call Jesus a prophet unless his or her eyes have been opened by the gift of faith.

From one standpoint, the third boundary is the most crucial, because after the man's parents refuse to get involved when the Pharisees question them about their son, the man is forced to assume full responsibility for his choices. The cowardly behavior of the parents becomes an asset to their son when the rulers of the synagogue confront him again.

The formerly blind man comes to the fourth boundary with an inner stamina that is very close to victory. Once again, we cannot miss the irony as the Pharisees bring the entire situation into the presence of God by putting the man under oath through the phrase, "Give glory to God!" By ranting at him, they introduce the man into the cost of discipleship; at the same time, his uncertainty changes into fuller conviction. He is able to withstand the taunts of the rulers of the synagogue and even to call them to face a moment of truth that could open up to them. It is an awesome moment when the man says, "Do not tell me you want to become his disciples too?" It is as though the once-blind beggar and the Pharisees are standing side by side on the brink of decision: for, or against, Jesus as Messiah. It is sobering, even terrifying, to watch them move off in opposite directions. Those who do not accept the truth regress. They become twisted and violent persons who throw the man out violently. Hence they are an image of those who refuse to accept the help of the Christ-life given in baptism.

Although insult and expulsion are harsh treatment, upon reflection the blind man, and we with him, will be able to realize that such confrontations become either occasions for growth or impulses to sin. The vain curiosity of the neighbors, the indifference of his parents, and finally the hostility of the rulers of the synagogue keep *them* hemmed in—locked in their current state. For his part, the man, while at first blissfully unaware, as he encounters each of the ensuing challenges, quickly learns that he needs courage to risk making the choices that bring him face to face with each provocation and closer to faith. Each time, he is able to keep the moment of choice from becoming an impulse to evil. This is what makes him an encouragement to the elect.

Jesus is present throughout the man's conflict. Jesus seems to be watching from a distance, and he reveals himself as soon as the once-blind man accepts the gift of faith. At first, Jesus exhibits himself subliminally—

present-in-his-absence—in a way similar to his manner of being present in the accounts of his resurrection appearances, as we will see later when we deal with the Gospels of the Easter season. Today's Gospel, then, represents an early theological reflection on the process of moving from unbelief to faith in Jesus. The author of John's Gospel ushers an historical event into the service of the theological reflection of the community of believers of which the author is a member.

In our own time, the proclamation of the account of the man born blind still serves to sacramentalize the presence of Christ in the celebrating community. This is a real and active presence of Jesus. When the questions "Who healed you?" and "Where is he?" are asked, they fan a conflict into flame within the believing community even as they did in the heart of the man who received his sight. When Jesus finally asks the definitive question, "Do you believe in the Son of Man?"[14] this conflict erupts into a word of personal dialogue: "Who is he, sir, that I [we] may believe in him?" The assembly hears Jesus answer, "He is speaking to you now." Therefore we too share in the living mystery of Jesus who is always available and inviting us to grow. The entire community is inwardly strengthened as it longs for transformation in the Easter passage.

The story of the man born blind is a paradigm of the process of growth in Christian life. We can identify with the man in today's Gospel as we journey toward ever fuller union with God. Again and again in the course of life we notice how the succession of displacements, adversities, disappointments, and the like stir up within us notions of new possibilities of how to respond to God. We need to affirm in faith these notions even before they are entirely clear to us. Often we struggle for a long time in darkness. Such periods of struggle can form trust, patience, and a host of other strengths within us. These in turn enable us to pass through successive stages of transformation. Such struggles and growth are the special, conscious content of the faith community's celebration on this Sunday.

First Reading: 1 Samuel 16:1, 6-7, 10-13

The First Reading tells the well-known story of how God sent Samuel to find a new king for the people of Israel. God chooses whom God wills, despite human expectations. God instructed Samuel to bypass the social norm of that period, that of choosing the eldest son of the family, who held the privileged place, and to choose the youngest instead. When David was anointed, the Spirit "rushed upon" him. In our day the Spirit-filled descendant of David, Jesus, will give the Spirit to those he will enlighten in baptism and confirmation in the approaching Vigil. Thus, like David we share in the mystery of being chosen by God, and we share in the mystery of Jesus, *the* chosen one, the beloved Son of the Father. We Christians are the "youngest son" whom God admits into the privileges of Israel in these last days.

The elect—and all of us with them—realize that they share in God's upsetting and transforming choice. The lowly state from which God delivers us is symbolized by the lowliness of David's role as shepherd, the meanest of occupations in ancient Israel. In our age the "low" condition is frequently felt to be internal, within our psyche. Many people labor under a burden of self-hatred because they have never felt the love of significant others in their lives. We need many Samuels today to proclaim to these "least of our brethren" the good tidings that God, *the* significant other, chooses them, and that God's favor rests upon them.

The tenor of the First Reading is that God's choice of David affirms the boy's natural gifts of grace and beauty *as a person,* not his birth rank. The anointing with perfumed oil, then, confirms all those good qualities in David that will make him an asset to God's people. The anointing also confirms God's choice. When the fragrant aroma of the perfumed oil surrounds David and sets him apart, he knows he is special and that God has liberated him from inner bondage that might have hindered him from responding fully to the mission God is entrusting to him. The language of the text says this vividly: " . . . and from that day on, the spirit of the Lord rushed upon David." These powerful words bring to mind the sacraments of baptism and confirmation, which celebrate God's strong and immediate action within those God has chosen.

Responsorial Psalm: Psalm 23:1-3, 3-4, 5, 6

The words of Psalm 23 are beautifully appropriate today as a response to the First Reading. Complete trust in our Shepherd engenders both the response and the refreshment to which he leads us. The Church has traditionally seen references to baptism in the verdant pastures and the restful waters. The "table before me in the sight of my foes" images the Eucharist, and the oil images the presence of the Spirit in the post-baptismal anointing, confirmation. Filled with the liturgy's nourishing Word, we sing of our own special character as anointed ones of the Lord. Surely only goodness and kindness will flow from a person so strengthened.

Second Reading: Ephesians 5:8-14

The reading from Ephesians is another example of Christian theological reflection. Following upon our chanting Psalm 23, it further enhances our sense of dignity as children of the light: "Light produces every kind of goodness and justice and truth." Note the declarative form. It is not an exhortation; it is a statement of what kind of action flows from our *being* children of the light. That is the contemplative stance. The language could not be more concrete and positive. As a matter of fact, those who have been baptized possess within themselves the power to arise from the dead and to act in the light of faith that Christ gives. We can only ponder in faith the life that the Holy Spirit creates when we encounter Christ. Gradually this life will permeate more of our being and shape more of our responses.

Second Scrutiny

The second Scrutiny follows the homily. Once again the Scrutiny celebrates in ritual what has been taking place through the power of the Word in the readings. The godparents/sponsors evoke great power each time they place a hand on the shoulder of the one they are sponsoring. Gestures are an important language, and they make an impact by giving "flesh" to our support and encouragement. They also create a *sense* of community. The intercessory prayers given in the ritual's text refer to freedom a number of times. The needs of the candidates, of their families, and of the whole world are included.

The first part of the Scrutiny's prayer of exorcism, the one addressed to the Father, emphasizes faith as the light of truth, and it prays that God will free the chosen ones from the falsehoods that surround and blind them. The gospel message holds pride of place in the Scrutiny, and the man born blind becomes a universal symbol showing us how sin antedates us and how helpless we are in the face of it.

> He [the man born blind] is surely an eloquent personification of the human experience of being caught in an evil not of our own making. What subsequent generations of theologians were to rationalize in terms of a doctrine of original sin, finds in this primordial biblical symbol a powerful expression. Evil is always prior to man, it is a condition into which we are born. Evil's radical origin is prior to the human condition. . . . This helplessness in the face of evil, this sense of being "caught" irrevocably

and irremediably—is the weight carried by the truly tragic figure of the *caecus natus* [the man born blind]. And because the passivity of the human condition is so much to the fore in this symbol, the divine initiative is inevitably thrown into sharp relief.[15]

The second prayer, the one addressed to Christ, is an earnest plea for those "who struggle under the yoke of the father of lies." The reference to the "men (and women) whom you have chosen for your sacraments" again stirs up our sense of anticipation and strengthens our ability to witness to the faith—even to the point of enduring martyrdom. The dismissal helps to make the candidates grow even more eager for full sharing in the communion that is the Body of Christ.

In the Liturgy of the Eucharist, we, the faithful, celebrate our own deliverance from the blindness of sin. Through the Scrutiny we enter into the mystery of Christ as head of his Body. In the Preface we sing the praises of the Son who came as man among us to lead us from darkness into light. As we make memorial of this action of Jesus within us, God—again *today*—rescues us from the slavery of sin and brings us to rebirth as children of adoption. Our praise-filled acknowledgment opens us to God's action in our midst and bids us join in the new song of creation. In such interchange our spiritual life grows.

Fifth Sunday of Lent: Death Becomes Opportunity for New Life

The celebration of the Fifth Sunday of Lent and of the third Scrutiny marks a high point in our anticipation. Today's liturgy grants us a hint of what the future will be like and a first glimpse into the land of promise. It is an inside view that assures us that we are walking with Christ either toward initiation or toward its renewal through growth in the spiritual life.

First Reading: Ezekiel 37:12-14

We will begin with the First Reading of the day and allow the celebration to build to its natural climax. The reading is an exciting word of promise. It speaks of bringing people out of graves and into their own land. It stirs up the longing for Christian growth. It arouses within us an eagerness to come into our native land, that is, into a mature relationship with God in the body of the Church. We will celebrate that relationship in the fast-approaching Vigil. We cannot hear the words "I will put my spirit in you" without becoming even more eager to celebrate the new life to be received or renewed in the sacraments of initiation. The reading helps us come to *know* that our human longings, symbolized by the land of Israel, are interpenetrated with the Spirit of God, who directs their fulfillment. In the power of the same Spirit we recognize the meaning of the words "I have promised, and I will do it, says the Lord," and we experience them truly as in-spirit-ing.

Responsorial Psalm: Psalm 130:1-2, 3-4, 5-6, 7-8

We respond to Ezekiel's message with the words of Psalm 130: "With the Lord there is mercy, and fullness of redemption." Chanted between the verses of the *"De Profundis,"* the words become a moving affirmation of hope. The cry for help proceeds from the depths of our innermost beings where we recognize the devastating power of sin. The psalmist leads us to resist sin's destruction by trusting in God. Our trust will not be betrayed, for we will see the power of sin broken by God's personal compassion.

Second Reading: Romans 8:8-11

In the Second Reading the Church proclaims the radical change that takes place in us through baptism. The words

"You are in the spirit, since the Spirit of God dwells in you" contain the power they proclaim.

Paul uses the terms *body/flesh* and *spirit* to describe opposite ways of living: the former meaning the unredeemed person, the latter standing for the one who has been redeemed in and through Christ.[16] Hence Paul equates body/flesh with sin and death, spirit with justice and (new) life. He sees baptism, the sacrament of Christ's death and resurrection, as the experience that puts to death the old life of the body/flesh and initiates the new life of the spirit. Nevertheless Paul admits that our struggle with sin is not over, even after baptism. At the same time, however, he attributes the entire gamut of human weakness—the habits of sin, remnants of sin, and sinful inclinations—to the body/flesh (unredeemed humanity) which, because of baptism, is now dead. Paul then assures us that this "dead" state has no power over us: We do not have to give in to it, since—again because of our baptism—". . . the Spirit of him who raised Jesus from the dead dwells in [us]."

Paul's words stir up our faith and hope that we need not remain in our graves, in those habits and attitudes that keep us from performing deeds of light. Even now our mortal bodies—all those unredeemed tendencies in us—will be brought to life through God's Spirit dwelling in us. In faith we know that by the Spirit we can perform deeds of life, and that is joy.

Gospel: John 11:1-45

If ever it is true that the Gospel makes the feast, it is true of this day. Even a cursory reading of this pericope from John reveals this. Its careful structure is not the analytical and clearly reasoned form of scholastic theology. Rather, it consists of a careful arrangement of several shorter narratives within the movement of the overarching story. Such arrangement enables us members of the celebrating community to "move around" within the story, to identify with some character or some movement in it, and to recognize that we are already living in the aura of the meaning we seek. In other words, the Gospel provides a moment of insight that greatly affects our growth in the Lord and invigorates our journey toward the Easter Sacraments.

The verse before the Gospel, "I am the resurrection and the life, said the Lord: he who believes in me will not die for ever" (John 11:25,26), serves as the major sentiment of the entire proclamation. It never allows us to lose sight of the mystery we are celebrating today. The words "This sickness is not to end in death; rather it is for God's glory" assure us right from the beginning that *our* sickness, our state of sinfulness (life of the body/ flesh) is not our end.

To catch the flavor of the story, we can look at the characters involved. As the story begins, we find Jesus and the disciples across the Jordan (John 10:40), away from the murderous plots of Jerusalem. The fearful, foot-dragging apostles have little inclination to return to Judea, and especially to Bethany, which was only three miles from Jerusalem. They must have caught their breath at the sudden burst of bravery on the part of Thomas: "Let us go along, to die with him." His willingness to die with Jesus parallels Peter's profession at the Last Supper, shortly before Peter denied Jesus. Secondly, Martha and Mary, Lazarus' sisters, both mildly reproach Jesus in their grief, "Lord, *if* [emphasis mine] you had been here, my brother would never have died." Finally, the members of the crowd join with Martha and Mary to ask, "*Why* could he not have done something?" (Emphasis mine.) The two sisters and the crowd exhibit forms of magical thinking; for them, the presence of Jesus would have warded off the death of Lazarus. They do not as yet have the power to see death as anything more than the tragic ending to all that life holds dear. They have no experience of the life beyond death—an experience that Jesus will bring.

Even though we, catechumens and faithful alike, are eager for the newness the Easter passage promises, we still identify with one or another of these characters. Thus when Jesus proclaims that he is the "resurrection and the life," he is speaking to us as well as to the crowd at Bethany. These words summon us to go with Jesus to the grave of Lazarus. There we are forced to acknowledge our sinful state, our lack of faith. At this point of recognition we know that any attempt to hide behind "If only" or "Why?" will be futile. The stark reality of our sins penetrates our consciousness when we hear that "Jesus began to weep," and even more poignantly when we hear him say, "Take away the stone."

The pain of our sinfulness contrasts with the tender compassion and the great personal power of Jesus when we see Lazarus respond to this twofold attraction and come forth alive at the words, "Lazarus, come out!"

The utter helplessness of Lazarus, even after he is recalled to life, gives us further insight into what we heard from Paul: Many effects of sin remain in us even after baptism. His helplessness also reminds us how the Christian community is expected to support its newly baptized members: by unbinding them, or, in current terminology, by engaging in enabling ministry to them. All of this forms part of the mystery, i.e., the divine-human reality, in which we share during our celebration of Word and Sacrament today.

Turning our attention to Jesus in today's Gospel, we notice that his action and his words reveal something that makes this Sunday the occasion it is. We puzzle over *why* Jesus delayed going to Lazarus. Such questioning helps us realize that this story deals with much more than a series of historical data.[17]

Oftentimes certain episodes in our life have meaning for us only long afterward. We may question and complain while we are suffering through certain experiences, but we may later recognize them as valuable when we can view them from the faith perspective of our entire lives. All the more is this true of the Christian community. It finds itself almost continuously in the midst of painful ambiguities and situations that bring death to innocent persons. Thus when we hear the apostles and others questioning *why* Jesus did not prevent Lazarus from dying, we are aware of other apparent inconsistencies in God's dealings with his people. We want to ask, "Why did God permit humans to disobey the most basic law of their existence, their dependence on God?" Reflecting on the birth of hope engendered within the disciples and us by the raising of Lazarus, we come to realize that death had to precede resurrection. That is the answer to our perennial "Why?" We also sense here a foretaste of the message of the Easter proclamation: "O necessary sin of Adam, which gained for us so great a Redeemer!" (*Sac.*, p. 186) Our journey toward our Easter passage, then, consists precisely in allowing this mystery of God's merciful providence to unfold within us.

The pain of bereavement that Martha, Mary, and Jesus endured over the death of their brother and friend provides insight into the Father's pain and compassion for sinners—for us who have died by sinning. We know that Jesus is now exalted at God's right hand and that he has received the "promised Holy Spirit" (Acts 2:33 NAB). We realize that the assurance we receive in faith is not that we will be brought back to mortal life. Rather, we will be raised to a *new* and *different* life. It is to us that Jesus says today, "I am the resurrection and the life," whenever, like Martha and Mary, we accost him with "Lord *if* you had been here . . ." or "If only things had been different!"

One final reflection on today's Gospel: Note that Jesus assures us that entry into the new life does not require physical death on our part: " . . . whoever is alive and believes in me will never die." The Church offers Paul's words from First Thessalonians 4:13-18 as an option in Masses for the Dead (*Lectionary*, #790.12). This passage includes the words " . . . we who live, who survive until his coming, . . . will be caught up with them [those who have died] in the clouds to meet the Lord in the air." Every exigency of our existence is to be brought into harmony with the new life given in baptism. Jesus, in identifying himself as "the resurrection and the life," indicates that he holds the trump card over death. The one way we can have such assurance in the face of death is to respond as Martha did: "Yes, Lord, . . . I have come to believe that you are the Messiah, the Son of God: he who is to come into the world."

In today's celebration, then, Jesus exhibits solidarity with and compassion toward all who are struggling under the grief caused by sin and lack of faith. He also takes the action required by the "deadly" situation in which we all find ourselves. He leads the way for us by enduring grief and pain, but he also plants the seed of hope. This hope will not be disappointed, for we hear the invitation "Come out!" New life, new motivation for our actions, comes to us with these words. Without this call to new life, we could not make choices for Christ and carry them out; but after we have heard it, we *know* the strength of the Spirit within us.

The Third Scrutiny

The third Scrutiny ritually expresses the call to new life we have heard proclaimed in the words of Scripture and in the homily. It is appropriate, again, that the Scrutiny's intercessions arise out of the needs we have recognized during the Liturgy of the Word—intercessions for the destruction of the power of evil, for the hope of victory, the desire for eternal life, and the longing for the Easter Sacraments. The first of the Scrutiny's prayers of exorcism is carefully constructed. (1) It begins with a laudatory address to the Father as God of the living; (2) it proclaims God's sending the Son to lead us from death to resurrection; (3) it asks for liberation of the elect from the power of evil that brings death, for their reception of new life from Christ, for their receiving power to bear witness to the resurrection; and (4) it does all this through Christ our Lord.[18] This prayer really comes alive if and when we recognize it as the voice of the

Church making audible Jesus' own words to his Father today. Standing before the tomb where sinful mankind has been interred, the Church addresses God as "Father of eternal life" and God "not of the dead, but of the living" (RCIA #178). Because it has already experienced the effects of Jesus' mission, the Church has the same sure hope as Jesus did: "Father, . . . I know that you always hear me." The Church *knows* that the celebrating community, both elect and faithful, will again be snatched from the death-dealing power of the evil spirit in the "close encounter" of today's celebration and even more completely in the celebration of Triduum and the Easter Sacraments. The second prayer, addressed to Jesus, is a clear expression of how aware we are that Christ is present among us as the one who liberates from death, releases from evil power, and communicates new life. All of this gives us a share in Christ's own resurrected life.

Preface of the Fifth Sunday of Lent

In the Eucharistic Prayer we express most fully what we have acknowledged in the Liturgy of the Word and in the celebration of that Word in the third Scrutiny. The words and gestures of the eucharistic sacrament take on a unique character today. They disclose meanings and release energies peculiar to the new life announced in God's Word. These energies propel us forward on our interior journey toward the Easter passage. Here again we find the "already" and "not-yet" dynamism of the Christ-mystery strikingly interwoven. We have found this reality—the being "present-and-yet-to-come"—expressed in the Gospel, in the words from Ezekiel, "I will open your graves and have you rise from them," in the "fullness of redemption" promised in the Responsorial Psalm, and in Paul's message that the Spirit is indeed dwelling within us. We celebrate all of this when, amid praise and thanks, we synthesize it into the simple narrative of today's Preface:

As a man like us, Jesus wept for Lazarus his friend.
As the eternal God, he raised Lazarus from the
    dead.
In his love for us all,
Christ gives us the sacraments to lift
    us up to everlasting life.   (*Sac.*, p. 405)[19]

Only the celebration of a faith community could create such power. No one but our Father, to whom our prayer is addressed, could generate in us the energies required to integrate the tensions that call us into a richer and fuller life: We have perished in sin and have been "restored." We have died and have come to life; we have arrived, yet still we press on to the finish. Our being mindful of the elect helps us also. We witness God's wonderful work in them; in them we long for full life in Christ. We are inclined to wonder: How there can be still more to come?

We are ready now to consider Passion Sunday, in which all the movements of our journey of faith thus far find their recapitulation and realization.

Passion (Palm) Sunday: Threshold to Triduum

The most striking and immediately evident detail about the celebration of this day—at once the last Sunday of Lent and the threshold to the Sacred Triduum—is that its movement is in reverse order to the sequence of events celebrated during Triduum. The order in the latter proceeds from death to resurrection. The order of this Sunday, however, begins with a sense of exaltation and ends with keeping memorial of the suffering and death of Christ. The feast as we have it today has grown out of centuries of Christian experience.

It originated in a variety of geographical areas representing a variety of responses to Jesus' Easter passage from death to life. The procession with branches of palm and/or other branches finds its origin in centuries of Christian practice in Jerusalem. In Rome, until the tenth century, the unique part of this day's celebration was the proclamation of the Passion; in Gaul the *traditio symboli,* or the giving of the Creed, was celebrated on this day. Out of that wealth and variety the Roman liturgy has forged today's celebration with its two parts: "Commemoration of the Lord's Entrance into Jerusalem," and "Mass." (See *Sacramentary,* pp. 122-126.)

Today's celebration contains a wealth indeed; it is a many-faceted jewel, a composite symbol of our being-in-the-world and, at the same time, of our becoming more fully Christlike. In our discussion of the mysteries of Lent we have called attention to the tension between the "already" and the "not yet" that is characteristic of the Christian life.[20] From this perspective, today's celebration is most appropriate for the final Sunday of Lent. We have been noticing foretastes of the Easter victory as we have moved through Lent; today's feast very strikingly projects Christian trust in the "happy ending" to life's vicissitudes. At the same time it keeps us mindful of the arduous way we Christians must travel with Christ. These characteristics make Passion (Palm) Sunday an appropriate gateway to the celebration of the Paschal Mystery during Triduum.

Instinctively the Church juxtaposes the polarities it experiences, and thus it builds a creative tension in us, a tension that almost propels us forward as we near our goal. The most succinct juxtaposition of opposites is "Hosanna!"—"Crucify!" The words come from the mouths of the same crowd. One greeted Jesus' entry into Jerusalem, his city; the other led him to his death outside its walls. The hills—Zion and Calvary—serve as opposite poles, and the sins of the former are redeemed by Jesus' sufferings on the latter. The city itself is ambiguous: It welcomes Jesus as Messiah, then hosts his death.[21] Actually, these opposites do not obliterate each other; each highlights the other. They make each other's existence possible, as do positive and negative areas in a painting.

Commemoration of the Lord's Entrance into Jerusalem

This part of the celebration focuses on Jesus' decisive action of entering Jerusalem—a victory for him inasmuch as he freely chose to do what he knew would lead to his death. Three options for celebrating this entrance are given in the *Sacramentary* (pp. 122-126): the first, with procession and solemn entrance; the second, the solemn entrance only; the third, the simple entrance. The first two include the blessing of palms and the proclamation of the Gospel that narrates the Lord's entrance into Jerusalem.

The brief introduction given by the presider emphasizes both Lent and our entry into the celebration of the Lord's Paschal Mystery. Both prayers for the blessing of palms refer to the palms as symbols of the honor we give to Jesus as triumphant King.[22] This blessing is followed by the gospel proclamation.

Gospel: Matthew 21:1-11

This Gospel seems almost a too-literal fulfillment of the Old Testament prophecy. Matthew quotes Zechariah:

> Tell the daughter of Zion,
> Your king comes to you without display
> astride an ass, astride a colt,
> the foal of a beast of burden.

Significantly, these words emphasize Jesus' humility by noting his affinity to the beast of burden. Jesus gravitated to the ass, a fellow bearer of burdens, and thereby won a new kind of victory. By allowing the populace to hail him as king and Messiah despite his lowly appearance, Jesus confounded those conquerors who enter vanquished cities astride prancing war horses or mounted on tanks or armored cars. In short, Jesus' victory identified him with the long line of defenseless people that stretches across the ages.

The Procession

The procession is deeply symbolic. The cross decorated with flowers and palms symbolize in advance the glory and beauty the cross has brought. Though we sing about the children of the Hebrews, we are also aware that we are members of Christ's Body who chant his praises on the way and at the same time anticipate our victory with him, particularly during the Easter Vigil, the climax of the Sacred Triduum.

The overarching symbol of this part of today's celebration is the threshold or entrance. Jesus is entering the New Jerusalem, the Church, where we will encounter in sacramental form his victory over the still-rampant powers of evil. As the faithful enter, they make their own passage into a new area of union with Christ; and the elect anticipate their entry into full membership in his Body, the Church.

The Eucharistic Liturgy

Our celebration is not unrealistic, for, like Jesus', Calvary also marks our passage. The mood of celebration changes dramatically as we enter into the Liturgy of the Word. The Opening Prayer sets the motif by phrases such as "model of humility," "giving his life on the cross," and "following his example of suffering." It also mentions the resurrection and acknowledges *hope* as an ever-present Christian reality.

First Reading: Isaiah 50:4-7

The third of the Suffering Servant songs is the First Reading for this day. It points prophetically to the kind of word that Jesus, as Messiah, will speak. It introduces us to the reason why Jesus suffered: "that [he] might know how to speak to the weary a word that will rouse them." The proclamation *effectively* calls us to enter into Jesus' behavior: not to rebel, but to give our backs to those who beat us, and not shield our face from buffets and spitting. Whether we must bear inner psychological pain or outer physical pain, we have God's promise that we will "not be put to shame."

Responsorial Psalm: Psalm 22:8-9, 17-18, 19-20, 23-24

Our dying with and in Christ lies at the heart of our victory. That is why we do not deny the real anguish in our lives. With our whole heart and soul we cry out in the Responsorial Psalm: "My God, my God, why have you abandoned me?" The verses from Psalm 22 take us through the intense sorrow of the redeemer and end with the victory he achieved through it.

Second Reading: Philippians 2:6-11

This familiar hymn epitomizes the entire plan of salvation—the entire Easter passage—from the incarnation, through Jesus' deepest humiliation, to the heights of exaltation. Since this selection is itself a hymn, every phrase is laden with meaning that influences us not only by its statements but also by its poetic form. The way the hymn is constructed helps the hearts of Christ's faithful to resonate with it. Contrast, or the juxtaposition of opposites, plays a significant role here. The power created by setting the opposing poles next to each other is clearly expressed in terms of movement, of passage. From the heights of his divine nature, the Son of God became human and descended even to the depths of death. This humiliation in turn motivated his Father to lift him to new heights. The artistic arrangement of the whole poem invites us to follow Christ in trust. The verse before the Gospel (Philippians 2:8-9) augments and reinforces this inner motivation by repeating the essential movements of the entire hymn: humiliation on the cross and exaltation by God.

The Passion: Matthew 26:14-27:66

The central motif of the day (indeed, of all Christian life) reverberates in the proclamation of the Passion of our Lord. We can say truly that all is contained in this solemn announcement. By taking a long, loving look at the action of the story we can move from being mere spectators to becoming participators in it. In this proclamation we discover that within the mystery of Jesus' dying lies the germ of salvation.

The discovery that salvation is inherent in God's response to human infidelity is, in fact, at the heart of the economy of redemption. The history of God's dealings with his people reveals this, and the account of the Passion is its highest expression, fulfilling all the prophecies and types that went before. The stark irony of releasing Barabbas and condemning Jesus to death must chisel the marks of God's love on the stoniest hearts. Jesus' plea for forgiveness is only apparently lost on deaf ears. One thief accepts the offer, and Jesus reveals to him the loving plan that the compassionate Father revealed at the moment when God laid on Jesus "the guilt of us all" (Isa. 53:6).

Preface of Passion Sunday

Such is the boundless mystery we celebrate this day. In the Preface of the Eucharistic Prayer we acknowledge our awareness of this mystery. In praise and thanks we say: "Though innocent, he accepted death to save the guilty," and even more, "By his dying he has destroyed our sins. By his rising he has raised us up to holiness of life" (*Sac.*, p. 411). These words are much more than a thank-you for the gift. They say that we have been carried into the heart of the giver, our Father, the all-powerful and ever-living God. We *know* that this ritual condensation of the story of the Passion makes it present once again. This act of making present is also a process that will carry us on to the Narrative of the Institution and Consecration, and still further, to the meal in which we share in the cup that could not pass away from Jesus. From the meal, the power spreads to our everyday life.

This threshold to Triduum, our annual celebration of the Paschal Mystery, signals our yes to God's offer of salvation. Lift up your hearts' lintels, O Christians! The King of Glory enters!

Although the RCIA prescribes no celebration of rites leading to initiation for this day, still the candidates for baptism are present to us visibly, and the RCIA does contain rites appropriate to celebrate this threshold stage of their journey. The Presentation of the Creed (RCIA #186-187) would be a most fitting part of this day's celebration, for, as we have seen, the liturgy concentrates within itself the entire work of salvation. The Presentation of the Creed allows elect and faithful alike to celebrate the significance that the death and resurrection of Jesus has for all who have set out on the conversion journey to Christ's Easter passage.

Summary: Another Loving Look

We have mentioned that in the Church the shape of conversion into Christ gradually came to be associated with the season of Lent and that it reaches its climax at Triduum, whose high point is the celebration of the sacraments of baptism, confirmation, and Eucharist in the Easter Vigil. Lent, then, not only affirms and supports conversion; it also celebrates its progress. The gospel passages we have been contemplating in this chapter present a primitive stage of that shape. We might compare these messages to hardy perennial plants—"capable of living over winter without artificial protection" (Webster).

Our purpose at this point is not to facilitate our "living ourselves into" the discoveries of earlier Christians but to highlight movements or life-lines that we have discovered in our contemplation of these Gospels and the other Scriptures that accompany them in the *Lectionary*. The first movement—that of purification—consists in turning away from sin and accepting Christ Jesus as Messiah. We recognize how Jesus' compassion helped the Samaritan woman accomplish such a metanoia. In the presence of the living water we also discover a symbol of baptism. By healing the man born blind, Jesus initiated the second movement, enlightenment. Arrival at full enlightenment indeed requires a struggle. We do not come to faith without letting go of many things upon which we normally lean for support. Finally, we find the third movement—the most thoroughgoing of all—in death to the old self and resurrection to a new mode of existence through the power of God's indwelling Spirit. All three movements are intertwined into our celebration of our journey into faith, which finds its summit and source in the Passion of the Lord.

We have seen that these Gospels are singularly contemporary in challenging us to grow. In the Gospel about the Samaritan woman, Jesus as Messiah initiates a dialogue not only with the woman but also with us to help us meet the challenges that come our way. By his own attitudes, Jesus invites us to let go of sexual and racial discrimination. Thus Jesus offers us inner personal strength in the struggles we may encounter, for example, in connection with the feminist movement and desegregation controversies. He also lends a sense of personal worth to those who are laboring under the burden of the divorce lure. Finally, hard-and-fast lines of demarcation between Christian denominations or between Christians and non-Christians will come tumbling down when we learn both to "understand what we worship" and to "worship the Father in Spirit and truth" (John 4:22, 23).

We also find timely calls to growth in the story of the man born blind. In our age of expanding social consciousness, we recognize the predicaments in which the blind man found himself after he had received his sight. Like him, we find ourselves amid frequent social changes that call us to scrutinize our commitments and to make some hard choices. Each significant social change becomes a boundary situation calling for transcendence, i.e., for moving beyond all present experience. Neither idle curiosity nor playing it safe nor violence will help us discover new frontiers in faith. Radical risks are required. In them, we come to discover Christ in our midst just as did the man born blind.

Although the story of Lazarus demonstrates that faith alone enables us to recognize the reality called resurrection beyond death, it does not deny the physical reality of death. Statements and questions such as "If only" or "Why?" are futile in the face of death. In fact, they divert attention from the sole giver of new life, Jesus Christ. Despite some illusions that death will be no more once our knowledge and our technology become sufficiently developed, the truth is that only in and through Christ can we ever become fully human, fully alive.

On the Sixth Sunday of Lent, when we celebrate the solemn entry of Jesus into Jerusalem in order to enter into his Passion, we reach the climax of the entire process of our conversion journey thus far. We have seen how the Samaritan woman, the man born blind, and Lazarus have become calls to faith for us because Jesus enabled them to say yes. The Passion Gospel proclaims the great choice of Jesus that brought him to his death and brings us the strength to grow. Jesus not only furnishes us with an example to follow. He also engenders within us the new-life power to join him. By joining Jesus we celebrate him as summit and source of the inner momentum of conversion and movement toward our Easter passage.

Finally, we have noted several times how story itself allows us space in which to move around. It allows the Spirit to breathe where it will in the heart of each hearer. Since it is the Spirit who readies each person to hear the Word, it is the Spirit who evokes new growth in the area that is already throbbing with readiness to respond. Faith and trust become the foundation for this process, and they build upon it as well. As we "rest" in the story process—including the Passion story—we do not try to force ourselves to grow; rather, we come to acknowledge that *all is gift*. Praise and thanks, commitment and intercession arise spontaneously from such acknowledgment. These responses in turn become incentives for further growth in our relationship with the Lord. In this way, they act as continuous inner forces that propel us toward the celebration of the Easter passage.

Notes

1. John Shea, *Stories of God: An Unauthorized Biography* (Chicago: The Thomas More Press, 1978), p. 183. The author uses these terms in a little different context. See Louis Bouyer, *Eucharist: Theology and Spirituality of the Eucharistic Prayer,* tr. Chas. U. Quinn (Notre Dame: Notre Dame Press, 1968), p. 34, where the author states, "The knowledge of God which results from the Word which is its preeminent fruit, a knowledge of which God is the object, itself proceeds from a knowledge that is anterior to the Word and which is expressed there: the knowledge of which God is the subject." This is expressed in the Preface for the Third Sunday of Lent: "When he asked the woman of Samaria for water to drink, Christ had already prepared for her the gift of faith" (*Sac.*, p. 401).

2. See Martimort, op. cit. The author of that section says that the three gospel passages in question were instruction to the catechumens in connection with the Scrutinies. These episodes from the New Testament were traditionally considered figures of baptism. On page 701, we find that the time of Lent, after having been limited to three weeks—the time of preparation for Easter—encompassed forty days by the end of the fourth century.

3. See a detailed description of this process in Henri Nouwen, "Compassion: The Core of Spiritual Leadership" *Worship* 51 (Jan. 1977):11-23.

4. See Raymond E. Brown, *The Gospel According to John I-XII* (New York: Doubleday, 1970), pp. 176-181.

5. See Brown, ibid.; also Ignace de la Potterie, *The Christian Lives by the Spirit* (Staten Island, N.Y.: Alba House, 1971), especially pp. 12-35.
6. The use of the relationship between father and son as a figure of the relationship between God and the Israelites appears frequently in the Old Testament. An outstanding example occurs in Exodus 4:22: "Israel is my first-born son" (JB). Others can be found in Hosea 11:1 and in Jeremiah 3:19.
7. All the circumstances of this story—water flowing from a rock, struck at God's command, and quenching the thirst of a rebellious people—converge to reveal the depths of God's gracious love. Water as the image of *wisdom* appears in Proverbs 13:14 (JB): "The wise man's teaching is a life-giving fountain" and again in Proverbs 18:4 (JB): "Deep waters, such are the words of man: a swelling torrent, a fountain of life." Isaiah invites all who have no money to "come to the waters," and later he compares the Word of God to the life-giving rain that does not go back to the heavens empty (55:1, 10-11 JB). Ezekiel sees water as the symbol of God's Spirit: "I shall pour clean water over you, . . . I shall put my spirit in you . . ." (36:25-27 JB), and Joel says: "I will pour out my Spirit on all mankind" (3:1 JB). Jesus reveals himself as the life-giving Word who quenches the thirst of every human heart:
    "If any man is thirsty, let him come to me!
    Let the man come and drink who believes in me!" (John 7:37-38 JB)
    To fulfill the Scripture perfectly he said: "I am thirsty," and to satisfy all human thirst he poured out from his pierced heart blood and water (see John 19:28, 34 JB).
8. See A. G. Martimort et al., op. cit., pp. 528-566.
9. See Robert D. Duggan, "Conversion in the *Ordo Initiationis Christianae Adultorum:* An Analysis and Critique," unpublished dissertation (Washington, D.C.: Catholic University of America, 1980), p. 156.
10. We experience some uneasiness nowadays about how to name the personal power of evil that we recognize as present in our lives. The juxtaposition of evil spirit and Holy Spirit in the prayer, however, helps us to make such an identification. The words quoted in the text are my translation of "Impera maligno spiritui, quem resurgendo

vicisti. Electis tuis iter ostende in Spiritu Sancto, ut, ad Patrem gradientes, eum in veritate adorent." (OICA #164)

11. Dugan, op. cit., p. 159 f.

12. This does not negate the power of other calls of God, e.g., in nature, in Sacred Scripture at other times, in private prayer, and the like. In fact, it celebrates all of these and makes them more intense.

13. Siloam was a pool at the southern extremity of the city of Jerusalem. In Isaiah 8:6 it symbolizes the hidden, peaceful protection of God. On the Feast of Tabernacles, waters were drawn from it and carried to the Temple as a symbol of the blessings of Messianic times. John's Gospel considers Jesus to be the one sent by God to bring these blessings. St. Augustine says: "The evangelist makes a point of telling us the name of the pool, and the fact that the name means 'Sent.' You already know who the 'One Sent' is" *Tractatus in Evangelium Ioannis* 44,2; quoted in Adrian Nocent, OSB, *The Liturgical Year* (Collegeville, Minn.: Liturgical Press, 1977), 2:109. Washing in this pool is an appropriate symbol of baptism, in which we are washed in the blessings Jesus brought us.

14. Note how the question asked of the once-blind man—and of us today—says as much by implication as it does by way of query. It is precisely as "Son of Man" that Jesus died. To believe in him, then, is to believe in his death and resurrection. Today is, in this respect, a foretaste of the Easter passage that we anticipate.

15. Duggan, op. cit., p. 165.

16. The first generations of Christians realized that, since they had come to know conversion in Christ, they experienced life as so radically *new* that they had to search for a vocabulary that would adequately express their "completely other" life. Thus when Paul, for example, speaks of new life he means the entire gamut of "radically other" experiences that came into his life with his conversion. The pair *body/flesh-spirit* is an example of words with a radically new meaning. Awareness of the phenomenon that came to be known as "Christian Latin" or "Christian Greek" has certainly been a help to alert the present writer to the faith realities that are spoken of in what seems to be ordinary language. For a description of this phenomenon see Christine Mohrmann, *Liturgical Latin:*

Its Origin and Character (Washington, D.C.: Catholic University of America Press, 1957); also see Mohrmann, *Die altchristliche Sondersprache in dem Sermones des hl. Augustin* (Nijmegen: Dekker en Van de Vegt, 1932); also A. J. Vermeulen, *The Semantic Development of Gloria in Early-Christian Latin* (Nijmegen: Dekker en Van de Vegt, 1956).

17. It seems to me that what looks like artificiality in Johannine dialogue is actually Christian theological reflection on the process of coming to know and accept Jesus Christ as Savior. See Brown, op. cit., pp. 287-329, for an excellent treatment of the Johannine dialogues.

18. It seems to me that by introducing the final sentence of the translations of the Roman prayers with the words: "We ask this," ICEL gives the faulty impression that Jesus is the mediator only of the petition part of the prayer. It is much more accurate to realize that both the laudatory address and the mention of God's wonderful deeds are being attributed to Christ's mediating power.

19. Although this Preface is theologically accurate and does contain references to the mysteries being celebrated on this day in the Liturgy of the Word, still it is hardly to be considered a *great* prayer. It lacks the elán born of identification with a meaningful liturgical celebration; it lacks an artistic touch.

20. See pp. 45, 46, and 74.

21. See L. Engels, "Hosanna, Zoon van David, de triomf van Palmzondag," *Tijdschrift voor Liturgie* 64 (1980):4ff, for an impressive commentary on Passion (Palm) Sunday.

22. This shows a significant shift from the mentality which looked upon the blessing almost as an infusion of power into the palms, enabling them to serve as protection against calamities.

4

THE PASCHAL TRIDUUM: THE MYSTERY OF THE PASSAGE AND ERUPTION INTO NEW LIFE

Overview

The shape of Triduum today exhibits many ·seeming ambiguities in its rituals. For example, they emphasize both historical episodes and sacramental encounters. That is why our celebrations may seem, at one and the same time, to mimic events of the past and to strive to grasp the fuller symbolic importance of each event. Nevertheless as we make the Easter passage each year and work to become more fully aware of God's eternal plan of salvation, these same ambiguities can lead us ever deeper into the many layers of meaning of Christ's Easter passage.

Pure chronology, historical time, and "God's time"—*kairos*—all influence one another during Triduum. "He suffered under Pontius Pilate" (Apostles' Creed) notes both the chronology and the historical time of the event that has dealt conclusively with sin and its effects. Since Jesus is both human and divine, his death and resurrection embodies both God's supreme act of compassion and the most completely human response. Jesus' passage, therefore, is the definitive breakthrough that tears down the barriers erected by sin and opens us to seek union with God. Jesus, as risen Lord, is no longer bounded by chronology nor by any specific era of historical time. Our sacramental celebrations carry us and our historical time into the *kairos*; in them we allow God to be God in our lives and times. During Triduum we tell the stories of the events of the last days of Jesus' mortal life, and we celebrate rituals that in the course of two thousand years have revealed the many-layered meanings those stories contain. In these rituals, Christ, now glorified, brings our confused lives and times into the victory and triumph of his Paschal Mystery.

If we realize that a personal attraction that is closer and more real to us than any other power in the world has addressed us, our reflective and seeking hearts respond with gratitude and praise. In the Eucharistic Prayer we celebrate such a high point of love. The Narrative of the Institution expresses in story form the heart of the Paschal Mystery:

> While they were at supper,
> he took bread, said the blessing, broke the bread,
> and gave it to his disciples, saying:
> Take this, all of you, and eat it:
> this is my body which will be given up for you.
> In the same way, he took the cup, filled with wine.
> He gave you thanks, and giving the cup to his disciples, said:
> Take this, all of you, and drink from it:
> this is the cup of my blood,
> the blood of the new and everlasting covenant.
> It will be shed for you and for all
> so that sins may be forgiven.
> Do this in memory of me. (EP IV, *Sac.*, pp. 558-559)

By narrating this story, we ritually make Christ's mystery of love present. The memorial acclamations that follow upon this central narrative also state the sum and substance of the Paschal Triduum: "Christ has died; Christ is risen; Christ will come again."

Finally, the Roman Calendar draws together the diverse elements that have gone into our present liturgical celebration:

Christ brought to completion the work of redeeming mankind and of fully glorifying God. He did this particularly through his paschal mystery, in which by dying he destroyed our death and by rising restored our life. This is why the Paschal Triduum of the Passion and Resurrection of the Lord stands out as the culmination of the liturgical year. . . .The Paschal Triduum of the Passion and Resurrection of the Lord begins with the evening Mass of the Lord's Supper, it has its center or high point in the Paschal vigil, and closes with the Vespers of the Lord's Resurrection.[1]

Thus, the Apostles' Creed, the Eucharistic Prayer, and the Calendar all inform us about the single movement that is the celebration of the Paschal Triduum. In brief, the following are the high points of celebration. In the evening Mass of the Lord's Supper we celebrate that final meeting of Christ with his disciples, with its emphasis on forgiveness. Even more significantly, we also celebrate Christ's gift of Eucharist, through which the Church makes present for all generations the great acts of divine compassion for God's people. On Good Friday we celebrate a ritual that both recalls and also brings us into contact with the historical event in which Jesus made the total and voluntary gift of himself and of the entire human race to his Father. The "quiet" Saturday allows the movement from humiliation to exaltation to take place. It is a time of expectation and is the "sacrament" of waiting for the return of the Bridegroom at the Parousia.[2] The great vigil celebration continues this contemplative mood of waiting even as it moves into the initiation of new members into the Body of Christ. This night is climaxed by our making present the Paschal Mystery in the sacraments of baptism, confirmation and

Eucharist. On Easter Sunday we celebrate with ecstatic joy the resurrection as culminating saving event.

As we look at each of the parts that make up this single movement from death to new creation, we constantly need to remind ourselves of its inner dynamic. Although its phases can be distinguished, they can by no means be separated. We do well to study each of them separately, however, in order to become more completely receptive to the entire movement of growth within the Easter passage.

Holy Thursday: Mass of the Lord's Supper

Since on Holy Thursday we are gathering to celebrate our communal and individual liberation through Jesus our Lord, who is the infinite compassion of God, the many allusions to the cross should come as no surprise. The Opening Antiphon evidences our cross-marked liberation. "We should glory in the cross of our Lord Jesus Christ . . . through him we are saved and made free" (*Sac.*, p. 135). This antiphon actually sets the tone for the entire Triduum and ties it together. We are truly celebrating Christ, "our *salvation,* our *life,* and our *resurrection.*" The Opening Prayer is a simple statement about the gift of the Eucharist. The prayer's petition, "that in this eucharist we may find the fullness of love and life" (*Sac.*, p. 136), also indicates that we recognize that the Eucharist itself contains the work of redemption—Christ's Easter passage—in ritual and sacramental form.

The similarity between the readings from Exodus 12:1-8, 11-14 and from 1 Corinthians 11:23-26 contains special meaning. Both describe rites in which God's people become present to divine saving action on their behalf. Several strands of tradition woven together compose the First Reading. This reading deals with the sacred meal in which the Israelites annually made passage to liberation. The selection from 1 Corinthians deals with the fulfillment of the exodus experience. By proclaiming it in juxtaposition to the exodus account, we can see how revelation developed and how the New Testament Word fulfills that of the Old Testament. This realization fosters hope and readies us to expect further development as we celebrate today.

First Reading: Exodus 12:1-8, 11-14

A closer look at this reading shows that it has much to teach us about faith development. When this text came into existence, shepherds practiced a widespread spring-time religious custom to ward off evil spirits from their flocks. They sacrificed a yearling lamb and sprinkled its blood around the enclosures where the ewes were giving birth to their young. Many Israelites were shepherds. Thus when they heard God addressing them through Moses, they used this familiar ritual to express their faith-response. As they sprinkled the blood on the door-posts and lintel of every house in which they were par-taking of the lamb, however, they recognized that they were doing more than trying to exert human power over demonic forces. They knew that they were saying a personal yes in trust and affection to the compassionate God who had addressed them. They were making the previous, incomplete religious symbol into a symbol *of their faith in Yahweh,* who had made them the chosen people and who was promising to set them free from the slavery under which they groaned. The blood of the lamb, then, looked back to something with which the Israelites were familiar, *and* at the same time it called them to transcend that familiar practice. Thus the symbolic gesture of ap-plying the blood to the doorposts looked to the future and called them to follow God unreservedly.

One part of the First Reading contains a special call to us in our day and culture. Note that God did not ask the entire community of Israel to eat together in one large group, but in small groups. The faith symbol itself, the lamb—not an outside force—determined the size of the group. Only if the household was too small to consume a whole lamb was it to join with another family to secure a sufficient number of people to consume the entire lamb. Thus the group would be neither too small nor too large. The family atmosphere could be maintained, and it in turn would facilitate communication and commitment. The lamb, then, would serve to nourish them physically and to bond them socially. The Israelites would need both physical strength and close-knit social ties for the ordeal they were about to undergo in crossing the Red Sea.

For Christians, the lamb slain and eaten becomes a ready symbol of Christ, the true Lamb of God, who died to take away the sins of the world and to gather us around his table of Word and Sacrament. Taking away the sins of *today's* world includes an act of gathering in a special way; it includes taking away the sins that bring about loneliness, isolation, and anonymity both in our places of living and in our places of worship. This is a dynamic "gathering" that engenders internal commitment through interpersonal communication. In our liturgical celebration the bonding that the give-and-take of dialogue engenders is a faith *commitment*, for it is precisely as *God's* people that we are nourished on this day. The more clearly we are in touch with the influences we exert on one another, then, the greater the effect of our celebration in our daily living.[3]

Attachment to God is always a journey, a passage. We can never entertain any illusion of settling down. Standing around the table with loins girt, staff in hand, and sandals on our feet is the only appropriate stance for us who respond to the Father's ongoing revelation.

Responsorial Psalm: Psalm 116:12-13, 15-16, 17-18

The response of the assembly to the First Reading proceeds from our Christian awareness that we now enjoy the fulfillment of the Old Testament: "Our blessing-cup is a communion with the blood of Christ" (see 1 Cor. 10:16). In the psalm, emphasis on the blood of the New Covenant is evident. The psalm amply reveals that the sacrifice is a sacrifice of praise[4] and that the human blood is that of God's faithful ones whose death is precious in God's eyes because it is united with the death of God's only-begotten Son.

Second Reading: 1 Corinthians 11:23-26

In the Second Reading Paul states that he has received from Christ the tradition he hands on. Few scholars doubt that the words Paul uses are from an Institution Narrative used in the primitive liturgy. Hence the *traditio,* in which "the victory and triumph of his [Jesus'] death are made present,"[5] is a ritual story celebrating the reality it recounts. It is the way that Christ has instituted for us to be present to him as he accomplishes the once-and-for-all sacrifice of praise to his Father. Christ's command "Do this in remembrance of me" proclaims this in so many words.[6]

Gospel: John 13:1-15

Today's Gospel begins: "Before the feast of the Passover, Jesus realized that *the hour* [emphasis mine] had come for him to pass from this world to the Father." Upon reflection, we see that *the hour* does not refer to chronology but to Jesus' own readiness and, above all, to the will of his Father. The Gospel places us in the presence of fulfilled time, into the reality of Jesus' personal self-offering to his Father for our sake. "He . . . would show his love for them to the end." Jesus loved, not only to the last moment of his earthly sojourn, but to the utmost limit of self-giving. As Christians we share the privilege and the challenge to do as Jesus did.

The Gospel makes it clear that if we want to do as Jesus did, we must see this day as much more than a "Day of the Blessed Sacrament," in the literal sense that expression often connotes. We have reflected a number of times on how the Gospel *makes* a particular feast. This day's celebration is no exception. If we take careful note of the way John describes Jesus' action, we will get an insight into John's concept of the meaning of Eucharist.

John's account of the institution of the Eucharist differs from those of the other evangelists and of Paul. Rather than dwelling on the words of institution, John sees the *total* meal as the essential symbol of what Jesus is doing. John says that Jesus rose from the table "during the supper" and took in hand not the bread or the cup, but a towel with which to wash his disciples' feet, even though, according to Jewish social customs, the washing of feet was out of place *during a meal.* John uses this anomaly to heighten our awareness that Jesus' action represented more than the act of hospitality ordinarily offered by a host to his guests through the ministration of a slave. John is telling us that in his heart Jesus is anticipating the humiliation (in death) that will forgive sins and offer us fellowship with him.

John then declares that after washing the disciples' feet Jesus *goes back to the table* before he asks, "Do you understand what I just did for you?" and speaks the injunction, "What I just did was to give you an example: as I have done, so you must do." In these words we hear overtones of Jesus' other "institution" command, "Do this in my memory." Our evening Eucharist evidently is the door to the celebration of the Paschal Triduum. Neither the washing of the feet nor the Eucharist can be considered apart from Good Friday and Easter, as we will see later.

Washing of Feet

In order to recognize the meaning of the washing of feet as we perform it in our assembly on Holy Thursday, we must first of all be attentive to the inner movements of our hearts as we listen to the Gospel. Secondly, we must be aware of the meanings that other Christians throughout the ages have experienced in this action. In the fourth century, Ambrose of Milan practiced the washing of the feet after the water bath of baptism.[7] Ambrose centered the practice on "having part with Jesus," and he saw the washing of the feet as completing the baptismal encounter with Christ. In the eighth century, we find an imitation of Jesus' action that parallels the gospel account: The bishop washes the feet of twelve poor persons. Although this rite was performed in conjunction with the eucharistic celebration, it added its own gospel reading just before the Preparation of Gifts. Still another influence that has a bearing on our practice today is that of the reconciliation of penitents, which for a long time took place on Holy Thursday.[8]

When we ask ourselves what is going on during the ritual of the washing of the feet, we do well to be open to each of the underlying meanings of the elements that influenced its development: (1) having part with Christ; (2) sharing in his humiliating death that washes away the filth of our sins and reconciles us to the Father; and (3) fraternal forgiveness, which is *our* way of laying down our lives for our sisters and brothers.[9] The antiphons suggested in the *Sacramentary* to accompany the rite of washing of feet indicate its essential meaning, since for the most part they are selections from the gospel text itself. They enable not only those who are physically involved in the rite but the entire congregation to be caught up into the sacred action.

Transfer of the Holy Eucharist

Reservation of the consecrated eucharistic species has a long history, but on this night it basically serves two purposes. First, the consecrated bread is destined for the sick and for distribution during the third part of the Good Friday celebration; for the Church has never celebrated the full eucharistic liturgy on Good Friday. Second, the reservation serves as the center of our devotion on this night of anticipation. The procession, which is usually done very simply, is a relic of the procession in the days when devotion to the Blessed Sacrament had all but replaced belief in any other mode of Christ's real presence on earth. Presently, the hours of the night watch provide us with an opportunity not so much to adore the Blessed Sacrament as to *watch and pray with the Lord.* Thus the *Sacramentary* terms this part of the Holy Thursday Liturgy a "transfer" (p. 139), indicating a thread of unity between this Triduum celebration and those to follow. The celebration of the *Pascha* has begun. Now the response to God is not made by Christ alone, but by Christ together with his Church, the spouse he has won for himself.

Additional Rites and Customs

It is not difficult to see how the day of the memorial of Jesus' washing the feet of his apostles has evolved also into a day for the Reconciliation of Penitents. Equally appropriate is the custom of providing in some way for the poor. Holy Thursday is a suitable "hour" for us as a community to become aware of the corporate injustice that has been, and still is being, perpetrated against the poor, and to recognize that social and political systems also have to be "converted."

Good Friday: Celebration of the Lord's Passion

By way of introduction to the texts for Good Friday, the *Sacramentary* states: "According to the Church's ancient tradition, the sacraments are not celebrated today or tomorrow" (p. 141). The celebration of Good Friday is indeed unique. Many varied strands of development have contributed to its present form. Therefore, only after describing some of the trends that have contributed to the form of our present Good Friday celebration, will we examine the three divisions of today's liturgy: (1) Liturgy of the Word; (2) Veneration of the Cross; (3) Holy Communion.

It is always hard to consider the dark side of the Paschal Mystery without becoming too simplistic or too pessimistic. Jesus has *de facto* conquered death and evil. We may be tempted to say that since evil has already been defeated, we do not have any responsibility to face evil realistically. On the other hand, we may be tempted to give up when we see the gigantic proportions that evil has reached today. Obviously, neither of these reactions is appropriate.

There is an inner relationship between the destructive force of evil that brought Jesus to the cross and the power in which he faced evil and then rose from the dead. "You hung him on a tree," Peter told his fellow Jews, "but God raised him up again" (Acts 2:23-24 NAB). The Messiah *had* to suffer these things in order to enter into glory (see Luke 24:26), Jesus told the two disciples on the way to Emmaus.

The Church faces that dark side of life today in order to confront the evil lurking in it. In grief and hope we contemplate the death of the Bridegroom. In doing this we are being quite realistic, because so much of human existence still resists redemption.

Already in the first century the Jewish converts to Christianity mourned their brethren who refused to accept Christ. They expressed their sadness by fasting from the day of the Jewish Passover until the following Sunday. Later in the Western Church, after the peace of Constantine, when interest in the sites where the work of redemption took place became widespread, a significant shift in mentality took place. Christians directed their sadness to the physical sufferings of Christ. They continued to keep a fast because it coincided with a mournful mood and because it prepared them for a more intense celebration of Easter. The cruel Passion came to be more and more romanticized, until numerous devotions to its successive phases—such as the agony, the scourging, the crowning with thorns, the carrying of the cross, and others—all but eliminated the healthy tension between the sense of sorrow over the personal evil perpetrated against the One sent to save us and the positive, palpable saving that Christ's suffering brought.

Our present Good Friday celebration not only displays something of this historical development in the West but also contains some elements from Jerusalem and from Greek traditions.[10] The mystery of the apparent triumph of evil thrusts itself upon our consciousness in stark realism. We stand together next to the present-day crucifixion of human persons in the multiform injustices of our age. As one author put it: "Modern suffering is like an endless way of the cross, a Good Friday on which the sun never sets"; and again, "Carrying the Cross of Christ is not something reducible to mere *metaphors*."[11] As we celebrate the memorial of the crucifixion today, we sense two realities. The first is that in the innumerable and apparently insurmountable evils in our world today we share in the crucifixion of Christ. For example, in faith we sense the crucified Christ's presence in a courtroom where an innocent man has been convicted, or in a country where many are starving, or in a nursing home where euthanasia is rampant. Secondly, we also know in faith that God is embracing all these evils, including our own, and is mysteriously transmuting them.[12]

We need to allow ourselves to be present to the crucifixion—the one on Calvary and its continuation today—in all its devastating reality so that our own root evil may not remain hidden and prevent us from hearing God. God did not require the shedding of blood; human beings did, as we say in the Eucharistic Prayer III: " . . . see the Victim whose death has reconciled *us* to yourself" (*Sac.*, p. 554; emphasis mine). In order to receive the full benefit of the impact of the death of Jesus of Nazareth, we make it present in Word and prayer, in ritual, in drama and song.

The Liturgy of the Word

Unusual atmosphere and gestures strike us at the very outset of today's celebration. The bare altar, the silent entrance, the prostration all represent an almost universal tendency to preserve ancient practices on the more solemn feasts and seasons,[13] and they engender a certain intensity at the opening of our celebration.

First Reading: Isaiah 52:13-53:12

After a brief prayer, and without any salutation or other introductory ritual formulae, the Liturgy of the Word begins. The first scripture proclamation, the Fourth Song of the Suffering Servant of Yahweh (Isaiah 52:13-54:14) contains several expressions of the tension between pain and growth, death and new life: " . . . it was our infirmities that he bore. . . . he was pierced for our offenses, crushed for our sins." Further on in the reading we hear the following passage juxtaposed to the one just quoted: "If he gives his life as an offering for sin, he shall see his descendants in a long life, and the will of the Lord shall be accomplished through him." Since *God* exalts the Suffering Servant—"I [God] will give him his portion among the great"—even the "hidden pitfalls that our sins present, open onto new fullness of being."[14]

Nowadays we may tend to overlook the value of Jesus' relationship to and dependency upon God. Many of us tend to rely on other things: on mathematical accuracy, on technical precision, or even on first-strike power. Unfortunately, none of these things touches what is most important to the human heart: relationship and personal intimacy. When we speak of doing the will of God or of entering into God's plan, we are not uttering childish fantasies as though we expect God to intervene and, with some super power, demolish all other forces. Rather, our doing God's will and entering God's plan reflects how much we value our relationship with God in love and trust even to death and beyond.

Isaiah compares the Suffering Servant to a lamb. As a *symbol,* this animal speaks volumes to the human heart. Its silence when led to slaughter and its quiet non-resistance when sheared have caused many to see in the gentle lamb a symbol of the human strength displayed by integrated persons who remain silent in the face of injustice and suffering. Recall what lovers will do for their partners, or what endurance parents exhibit at the bedside of a sick child. On the faith level, this strength points to the sustaining power generated in a human person by reason of his or her intimacy with God. Think of the long, drawn-out torture that martyrs are able to endure. We know how Jesus in his Passion displayed such power too. In fact, in the face of his strong silence the high priest grew annoyed, Herod became enraged, Pilate wondered—caught his breath, as it were, and asked again, "Where do you come from?"

Responsorial Psalm: Psalm 31:2, 6, 12-13, 15-16, 17, 25

Just as the liberation of the Israelites from the slavery of Egypt was crowned by their being called to be God's special people, so too, the climax of human salvation is revealed in this Servant Song as being a call to, and the accomplishment of, intimate relationship with the ever-faithful Father. The reading from Isaiah points to that intimacy by insisting that the Servant is doing the will of God. The Responsorial Psalm and its antiphon reiterate this close bond: "Father, I put my life in your hands" (see Luke 23:46). "I am forgotten like the unremembered dead; I am like a dish that is broken. But my trust is in you, O Lord." Such faith, trust, and affection enable us to plead: "Let your face shine upon your servant; save me in your kindness."

Second Reading: Hebrews 4:14-16; 5:7-9

The selection from the Letter to the Hebrews seems to have been deliberately spliced together to fit the assembly's need on Good Friday. It brings Jesus' role as high priest to bear on the tension and sufferings that human beings *know* on this day. As a man, Jesus knew how to cry out for help. In so doing he not only gave us an example to imitate, but he also made himself the *Way* through whom we can enter into the saving mystery of the crucifixion.

Gospel: John 18:1-19:42

John's account of the Passion is perhaps the one that most vividly portrays how our loving God embraces evil and uses it to reveal the sin that lurks in human hearts. It reveals how evil becomes entangled in the very web it has woven and is laid bare right at the heart of the greatest sin ever committed. Jesus, against whom the sin is perpetrated, turns the tables and reveals how those who condemn him to death are themselves condemned by their own judgment.

The gospel pericope is a masterpiece not only of Christian faith-witness but also of literary composition. Regarding the latter, John's use of effective juxtaposition of opposites and penetrating irony makes the account all the more effective. In the trumped-up trial before Annas, for example, Jesus defends himself and calls Annas and his minions to live in truth. John situates this trial between two episodes of Peter's denial, which takes on an added hue when contrasted with the way Jesus' accusers denied him. We find another example of irony in the Jews' refusal to enter the praetorium so as not to sully the ritual purity required for them to partake in the Passover meal. At the same time, however, they violate their identity as God's people—which the Passover meal celebrates—by condemning an innocent man to death and by publicly declaring that Caesar was their king. Again, Pilate's attempt to save Jesus through compromises only goads on Jesus' enemies.

It is noteworthy that even in the midst of his deepest helplessness and humiliation Jesus is able to declare his kingship, his devotion to truth, and his choice to die. He stands before a temporal authority, clothed mockingly as king, his death demanded by the people he loves, held captive though a criminal is released, his deepest mission apparently hopelessly frustrated. Even in this state, Jesus tells Pilate plainly that he is a king and that his "kingdom is not of this world." He witnesses to *truth* as the goal of his mission. He makes it clear that he freely chooses to go to death and that others possess power to use against him only because it is given to them from above. Thus his Passion is truly a "glorification," as he said it would be (John 17:1; 13:31-32). It is the tool God used to demonstrate divine greatness breaking the bonds of the flesh. The chief priests pass judgment on Jesus, and they prod Pilate to ratify their false condemnation, but in that very act the tables are turned on them, and their sin is made manifest. Truth and judgment triumph in that moment. Even the superscription placed on the cross proclaims Jesus' kingship.

Jesus' *inner* power is further seen after he is lifted up. He watches the soldiers throw dice for his seamless robe. He addresses Mary as "woman," the new Eve and mother of all the living (see Gen. 3:20). He fulfills all that the Scriptures have said of him, and he freely delivers over his spirit. The *act* of infinite love has become the eternal *sign* of boundless love.

Two final and very important observations need to be made. The first is that John highlights the blood and water that flow from Jesus' side. We find evidence in early Christian literature that Christians in their theological reflection sensed the water and blood to be symbols of sacramental encounters. In these encounters—particularly baptism and Eucharist—the event that happened in time (Christ's saving death) was seen as eternal. St. Augustine even says that "the church as the new Eve came forth from the side of Christ the second Adam, asleep in death on the cross."[15]

The second observation is that John quotes from Zechariah 12:10: "They shall look upon him whom they have pierced." This passage has much to say to us, both to help us in our present needs and also to teach us how Jesus' death becomes our salvation. When we look directly at someone we have harmed and see the suffering we have caused, there is a chance that we will be moved to human compassion. Compassion in turn paves the way for contrition. Unfortunately, humans today often perpetrate indirect piercings and killings—abortions, bombings, stealing raw materials from so-called under-developed countries, and more—and they do *not* have to look upon the ones they have pierced. Consequently, they miss an important human impetus to compassion and repentance. No one feels guilt, and inhumanity continues unchecked.

John's reference to Zechariah also grants us insight into the salvific power of Jesus' death, which plants the seed of a new and different life in the dark soil of human sin. The Messiah *had* to suffer and die. And as we look upon the all-holy sinless One whom we have pierced, we identify with him and really enter into him. Through his death we come to recognize that, as the prophet Nathan revealed to David, "You [we] are the man" (2 Sam. 12:7 NAB). In Christ crucified—the unique self-gift of a human being to the Father—we learn how we have killed ourselves by becoming unfaithful lovers.[16] But also in Christ's death we return with him to the loving embrace of our Father, and we exclaim, "By dying he destroyed *our* death!"

General Intercessions

Through the new insights and love power that have been engendered by contemplating the Word of God, we pray the General Intercessions and join Christ in his present role as intercessor. Thus when we pray for the needy ones, we are performing the Church's most precious form of ministry: drawing those for whom we pray into the all-embracing love of God.[17]

Veneration of the Cross

Even if we are unable to verbalize what is going on within us as we kneel and sing "Come, let us worship" during the threefold Veneration of the Cross, still we sense intuitively that our entire existence is centered on the cross. The act of kissing the cross articulates a variety of emotions: sorrow, hope, affection, grief. The Church does not expect it to be a morbid act, though; the first chant suggested in the *Sacramentary* is a clear expression of the Easter joy that has come to us through the cross:

> We worship you, Lord,
> we venerate your cross,
> we venerate your resurrection.
> Through the cross you brought joy to the world.
> (*Sac.*, p. 159)

The verse "May God . . . let his face shed its light upon us" (Ps. 66:2) speaks of our affectionate trust in our compassionate Father. God alone can scatter the darkness of sin symbolized by the darkness that covered the earth from the sixth to the ninth hour. The plaintive chant "My people, what have I done to you? How have I offended you? Answer me!" marks a strong contrast to the more vigorous

> Holy is God!
> Holy and strong!
> Holy immortal One,
> have mercy on us! (*Sac.*, p. 160)

The varied moods evident in the Veneration of the Cross are expressions of the varying experiences of the people who celebrate—people who feel the frustrations as well as the hope symbolized by the cross of Christ. They *know* the reality of suffering and death in their lives. Often in the depth of their existence they find themselves to be at cross-purposes. Life makes so many contradictory demands it may be difficult to determine where the mystery of the cross is more truly present—*incognito* in the goings and comings of the secular society, or *recognized* in the dramatic stirring liturgies in our churches. Good Friday is the time to reflect and integrate the two.

Holy Communion

The 1955 calendar revision introduced the Communion Service into the Good Friday celebration. Although this practice is a more satisfactory arrangement than the former "Mass of the Presanctified," we tend to agree with A. Nocent, who regrets the custom[18] because it detracts from the climactic eucharistic meal of the Easter Vigil. Even though the Eucharist is always the sign of our sharing in the death and resurrection of Christ, still we lose some of the intensity of our hunger and longing for the sacrament as the climax of the Vigil by taking what might be called a "snack" on Good Friday.

Holy Saturday: The Time of Passage

A. Hollardt, OP, calls the second day of the Paschal Triduum the day of forgotten mysteries.[19] A potential wealth of divine and human growth is contained in the mourning and anticipation experienced on this day. To enter into the day's full significance for us, and to see today as the occasion of passage from death to resurrection, we will consider its impact on three levels of human experience.

On the level of what is perceptible to the senses, we can consider the grain of wheat: "Unless the grain of wheat falls to the earth and dies . . ." (John 12:24 NAB). During the time when the moisture in the ground and other conditions that encourage decay affect the grain of wheat, the seed seems dead, just rotting away. Yet something very important, even essential, is happening. It is becoming plant food for new life. The content of the seed in its hard state could not enter as food into the new sprout. If the seed could think and choose, it would be faced with a very hard choice indeed. It would have to risk its entire existence for the sake of a new life of which it as yet has no experience. Its alternative would be to decide not to let this happen. But then it would remain just a seed, at least until it disintegrated entirely. This analogy speaks about what is happening during the quiet time of Holy Saturday.

Pious Catholics certainly notice that there is nothing going on in church today. Probably very few realize why this is so. But the Church is telling us that we need *time* for quiet thought and meditation in order to feel, to sense, what is happening as the Church moves from grief over sin and the death of Jesus to anticipation of forgiveness and new life to be celebrated during the Vigil. At present, few of us realize what the Paschal Fast entails, and since we have not learned how to subordinate last-minute shopping, cleaning, visiting, or even "business as usual" to our need for inner quiet, we are in danger of remaining "just a grain of wheat" and never really making sense of the full joy that new life offers.

The second level, where human experience surpasses what the senses can perceive, also gives us insight into the significance of Holy Saturday. On this level we tend to ask questions such as, Who am I? Why do I exist? Why am I such as I am? Where do I come from? Where am I going? On this level, too, many dark and deadening happenings take place. Periods when we are confronted by evil, failure, even sin, are darkened by anxiety, fear, anger, and guilt. We face a choice here: Either we admit these dark, painful emotions and risk being destroyed in the process, or we continue in a life of superficiality. To make such choices, we have to give ourselves sufficient *time* to work through them, for integration does not happen instantaneously. During the time it takes to deal with denial, anger, bargaining, and depression, nothing may seem to happen as far as integration goes.[20] Oftentimes, our pain becomes worse before it gets better. Nevertheless, because of the choices they entail and the pain they cause, situations like these help us recognize that new levels of being arise only from the death of old levels. And that understanding helps us understand the meaning of the Holy Saturday event and opens us to experience its dynamic in faith.

The third level on which this day makes an impact is the level of faith. On this level, we profess in the Apostles' Creed: "He descended into hell," and further, "On the third day he arose again from the dead." Though the other two levels of human experience support it, the faith level moves us beyond them. Scripture records how the faith level came into play immediately upon the death of Jesus: "That was the Day of Preparation, and the sabbath was about to begin" (Luke 23:54 NAB). The hurried burial of Jesus is the external circumstance that ushers in the great sabbath of the Lord. This sabbath begins in sorrow and grief for Jesus' followers, but it is neither a repeat of Good Friday nor just a vacuum before the resurrection. The day initiates and brings to fruition something very important, even essential, for our salvation. Jesus' acceptance of being *dead* is his lowest humiliation and the depth of his self-emptying. While his body lies three days in the grave, he is personally present to the dead in the "bowels of the earth."[21]

As part of the Paschal Mystery, Jesus' descent into the grave is the exemplar of our burial with him in the waters of baptism. For Christians of the third to sixth centuries Holy Saturday was the day on which they celebrated final exorcism of the catechumens and anointed them with the oil that prepared them for their definitive struggle with the powers of evil in the waters of baptism. For the faithful, this hiddenness in the grave exemplifies our entire Christian life hidden in Christ and with Christ in the Father. His rest in the grave sanctifies our graves. His descent into the realm of the dead gives us the joy of maintaining hope for victory even when we realize that we are in the throes of an evil we cannot defeat.

Holy Saturday, then, is the time when salvation is working itself out as the passage from death to life in the resurrection. If we see salvation in this light, we can have the strength to remain resolutely in touch with ourselves or with others, even if either we or they are denying, angry, bargaining, or depressed. It is all right to be "on the way," provided we do not choose to "sit down on the way," as it were. It takes patience to be with Jesus in the abode of the dead and to allow him, in his own time, to break the chains of evil and to trample down the gates that keep us prisoners.[22] For our part, we need constantly to call out to Christ our Savior, inviting him to be with us where we are delayed in our own particular abode of the dead. At any stage of our imprisonment we represent the Church in its present state. Though it is sinful, it is turned entirely toward the risen Lord, whom it awaits confidently, always expecting him to come and take it with him to freedom.

Far from being an a-liturgical day, in the sense that it is a "free day" with nothing going on in church, Holy Saturday is a day of movement from death to new life. It celebrates an important reality of human life: growth through death, or gaining new life by losing old life.

Looked at from another angle, Holy Saturday is a day of keeping expectant watch beside the grave, while growth toward readiness for the resurrection is going on within. It is a day of the Paschal (Easter) Fast. The *Constitution on the Sacred Liturgy* calls for the reinstatement of the Paschal Fast: "Let the sacred paschal fast be observed everywhere on Good Friday and where possible, let it be prolonged throughout Holy Saturday" (#110). In its recent calendar revision (1969) the Church prolonged the fast until the beginning of the Easter Vigil. This is indeed the great fast, at one time meant to last the forty hours that Jesus remained in the tomb. The Paschal Fast is not an addition to the lenten penitential fasting. There is something deeper and more intense about it. It is an expression of sorrow that the Bridegroom has gone away, but it is more. In one sense, it represents the Church's essential stance, even its identity. The Church remains turned entirely toward the risen Lord, waiting for the Bridegroom's return, even while it is struggling in uncertainty and sin.

It has been a universal custom in both East and West not to celebrate the Eucharist during the Paschal Fast. This custom makes the Paschal Fast the eucharistic fast par excellence. This fast helps us get in touch with our hunger for the eschatological banquet of the Lord. Liturgically, it creates a yearning and a readiness for the climax of the great Vigil. On the level of our senses, the longer we fast the hungrier we get. On the level of our human awareness, the more we allow ourselves to acknowledge the pain in the dark areas of our life, the stronger becomes our motivation to work through them. Finally, by incorporating the effects of these two levels of perception, our faith leads us to be more open to recognize our sinfulness and helplessness and to call upon Christ for salvation.

By celebrating Holy Saturday in full consciousness of what we profess in the Creed ("He descended into hell") and with the support of the Paschal Fast and of abstinence from the Eucharist, we ready ourselves to relish the eucharistic banquet more and to celebrate it with fuller commitment as the climactic celebration it is meant to be. By no means, then, is Holy Saturday an a-liturgical day. An intense spiritual activity is happening. And the Paschal Fast is the unique, common, symbolic gesture that expresses it.

The revised Liturgy of the Hours for Holy Saturday captures the day's spirit quite well. The Opening Prayer concentrates in itself the whole vision of the day:

Almighty, eternal God,
    your only-begotten Son has descended into the
        depth of the earth,
    from whence he has risen in glory.

> Graciously grant that your faithful
> who have been buried with him in baptism
> may through his resurrection
> make progress on the way of eternal life.
> Who lives and reigns with you. . . . Amen.[23]

Some new antiphons and readings in the Liturgy of the Hours also capture well the spirit of Holy Saturday. All in all it is a liturgy of hope. It gives an authentic vision of the descent of the Lord into the realm of the dead as part and parcel of the paschal happenings—of the Easter passage—for the salvation of human beings. Holy Saturday, as a day of passage through death to life, summarizes the full Paschal Mystery, which in essence is the passing over from humiliation to exaltation.

The Easter Vigil: The Climax of the Journey

We have already noted that a movement from bondage to freedom, from death to life, takes place over the long day of the Bridegroom's absence. On Holy Saturday, ever so gradually we realize within our own hearts that Jesus is "free among the dead." From Jesus we receive courage to submit our own sinfulness to his healing power. We sense how radical must be the yes we say to him as we move nearer to the goal of the journey we have been traveling since the beginning of Lent. Almost imperceptibly we are readied, together with the whole Church, for our entry into the celebration of our final "breakthrough" in Christ. In fact, this maturing process becomes fully apparent only when it is celebrated.

This night of vigil summarizes the entire process of creation and of salvation in the lives of those who come to celebrate. The conversion journey of each person present is caught up into the life stream we celebrate in the primordial symbols of fire and water, light and darkness, nakedness and white garments, hunger and abundant food, death and life, Word proclaimed and responded to. We need sharpened senses to see what the

Church is showing us, to hear what it is saying, to perceive the aromas it senses in faith, to taste the food it
offers, and to thrill at the touch by which it calls us to
life. The Church needs to deal in symbols, for the reality
we call into being in the vigil celebration lies beyond
human clarity on any level, physical or psychic. Who
could enclose in any human words the rich meaning of
our relationship with the God whom Jesus taught us to
call Father? This intimate relationship is bound up with
what Christ, God's Son and our Lord, has accomplished.
By his passage through death he has become "life-giving
Spirit." In the words of Louis Bouyer:

> Through the power of His Cross, now triumphant
> because of His resurrection, all people are to un-
> dergo a cross which will not be some other cross,
> but rather their participation of His, so that they
> may become *partakers of His own resurrection.*[24]

We cannot insist too often that as we celebrate the Vigil
we are caught up into Christ's own passage from death
to life, and thus it is truly "our own mystery that we are
celebrating."[25] We share in the entire history of salvation,
as the *Constitution on the Sacred Liturgy* affirms: "The wonderful works of God among the people of the Old Testament were but the prelude to the work of Christ the
Lord in redeeming mankind and giving perfect glory to
God" (#5). To understand this night of "breakthrough,"
we need to contemplate the various symbols we use to
celebrate the Paschal Mystery this night.

The Service of Light:
Our Celebration in Light and Lyric

On this night God continues to reveal himself as creator
and redeemer. Cosmic powers serve very well as symbols
to carry us into the secret working of God within us. We
begin in darkness and allow that darkness to speak to
us of the inherent danger of our reverting to the chaos

that sin causes. Our hope is "stretched" and strengthened, however, by the opaqueness of the dark. The spark from the flint is a ready symbol of that hope which, as we have seen, lies buried within every "curse" from Paradise to Calvary.[26] The cry from the cross broke all the fearful sound barriers of sin; and Jesus "delivered over his spirit" as he bowed his head in death. Now in the spark that flies out into the darkness when the flint is struck we recognize the Spirit released within each praying and fasting community of the universal Church. Once released and caught, the spark becomes a blazing flame of new fire, signaling the light of faith the Spirit kindles.

The presider breaks the silent darkness with an introductory remark. He then speaks a blessing in the presence of the fire, a prayer replete with images that are universal in the life of the Church. The prayer speaks of our share in God's glory and of Christ the light of the world. It petitions God to inflame us with new hope, to purify us by this Easter celebration, and to bring us to the feast of eternal light.

The presider lights the Easter candle from the new fire, and the flame, breaking the darkness from atop the large column of wax, easily evokes our remembrance of the pillar of fire that God provided for his people at the Red Sea and in the desert. The lighted candle also symbolizes the light and life of faith that Christ brings us.[27] Words, melody, the threefold gradation in pitch, and especially the awed, silent pauses during which we watch the light spread from the large candle to the many small ones, all contribute to the total effect of releasing a spiritual energy that is both human and divine. All of this serves to create an environment in which the meaning of Christ *as our light* can be caught and felt even as the flame of the candle is caught.[28]

The Easter proclamation, or *Exsultet,* is just that: a manifestation of an inner experience. The joy that erupts in this text could never be put on from the outside; it has to be a spontaneous utterance overflowing from the exuberance within the celebrating community. To derive the full spiritual value from the *Exsultet,* we must simply hear and admire the phrases that strike home and allow those insights that move us to resonate again and again (*Sac.,* pp. 182-184). It may be that we are captivated by the phrase "this is the night" as it reiterates the *presence* of salvation; or we may be overwhelmed by such bold contrasts as "to ransom a slave you gave away your Son." Again the exhilaration involved in proclaiming, "O happy fault, O necessary sin of Adam,"[29] brings to a climax and to full view those glimmerings of paradox that we have noted earlier during Lent.[30]

This opening tableau of the holy night is realism in artistic form. The strong contrasts emphasize the conflict between Christ and the powers of darkness. By artistically portraying the greatness of divine mercy, this tableau also highlights the seriousness of sin. All of this enhances the triumph of the compassionate love of the Father. No evil power can hold out against love's advances. We could say that the Vigil opens with a sight-and-sound collage that sets the mood; we notice too that the entry into the "vigil of all vigils" is a prime example of a spirituality that simply admires God as being wonderful in what God does;[31] and it follows that this spirituality is one of hope and joy.

The catechumens—and the faithful also—have long been waiting for the Light of Christ to illumine them by the gift of faith. This anticipation is an important aspect of the Christian life, for it indicates that we realize something new is straining to come to birth within us and that we are ready to welcome it. For those of us who have been baptized, some areas of our lives may have remained in darkness for many years. In such cases the darkness is real and blots out entire areas of potential growth. In God's own time—a fullness of time—our merciful God, by sharpening our inner conflicts and creating a sense of dissatisfaction within us, calls that hidden potential into active being. In this way God "causes" the conversion process to begin all over again. When such re-conversion has come to term, a birth takes place and causes joy to break forth in the same way that initial conversion does.

Liturgy of the Word: Our Family Album

Whenever human persons, individually and especially as a group, arrive at an important insight, they tend to reflect on the process that brought them to that stage of growth. They need to ponder it in order to understand and to firm up its impact on their total history thus far. The Christian community is no exception in this regard. The celebration of the new light not only provides an entrance into the event of the holy night, but it also makes present, in a symbolic way, the entire mystery of God's merciful love and human salvation. After the lighting of the fire, the assembled community enters into a long period of quiet, contemplative dialogue with the Lord. We take a long, loving look at the events that have brought us as a people thus far. We proclaim our amazement at God's wonderful deeds, admiring God in each, and we enter again into the dialogue that each event engenders.

We celebrate the Liturgy of the Word on this night in the same manner as we do on any other occasion. It takes the form of dialogue, or more precisely a dialectic of call and response between God and his people. On this night, enthusiasm is high. We expect so much. The Holy Spirit is symbolized—is *actively present*—in the back-and-forth movement of the dialogue. Together, as God's family, we listen in faith, and in faith we respond to God and to one another.

The content or topic of this contemplative dialogue could be viewed as being our family album. The nine scripture readings in our *Lectionary* are not play-by-play accounts of every occasion when God's people allowed God to be God for them. They are not even the only possible series of readings. But the texts do provide us with sufficient proclamation to enable us to enter into the movement of salvation history and to experience the continuity and growth of our covenant relationships.[32]

A note in the *Lectionary* explains that for pastoral reasons the number of Old Testament readings may be reduced. We must be on guard lest we consider shortening the service as having absolute value. We have pastoral needs that are far more urgent than "saving" of time. One of these is to understand experientially what is meant by "corporate" history. Sometimes we consider the Liturgy of the Word on this night as the final and recapitulating catechesis for the elect. It is this and more.

Proclaiming the Word of God always has two aspects:

Preaching the Good News to awaken the response of faith in the new message is kerygma. But the kerygma written down and proclaimed repeatedly in the liturgical assembly to recall us to our commitment to the Good News already heard and accepted in Faith . . . is anamnesis.[33]

By and large, we have emphasized the kerygmatic force of the Word during Lent, and during Triduum the emphasis has been more fully on anamnesis, or remembering and making present amid admiration and praise. A moment's reflection will reveal how the two are always intertwined. On this night particularly we notice how each praise-filled proclamation is a new call to conversion and deeper commitment to God in Christ.

On this holy night we have a pastoral need to follow salvation history, step by step. We need to savor the entire process and take a long, loving look at the events, and we must be careful not to omit any of them, for each one is a precious gift from God. We also have a pastoral need to discover ways of allowing *all* to assume some of the responsibility for helping one another to enter into each event in faith, to savor it and to allow God, once again, to "give the increase" as we make memorial of each wonderful deed. In this way salvation will become a mutual enterprise tonight. God awaits the fullness of time, and the master must find us ready when each event is proclaimed.

Let us now reflect on each of the pericopes, together with its response and prayer. Needless to say, anticipation colors the entire period of contemplative dialogue.

First Reading: Genesis 1:1-2:2

In the twentieth century, as we recognize our dangerous power to bring on a cosmic cataclysm, the magnificently poetic account of the first creation contains some striking calls to conversion as it recounts the wonderful deeds of God for our admiration. The refrain "And God saw that it was good" may seem like a voice crying in the wilderness of our anxieties. The dangers of global war and destruction are compounded by the fact that so few persons are able to affirm their own goodness, either psychologically or spiritually.[34] Our condition approaches that of "a formless wasteland." But amid this darkness and our near-despair, God proclaims that he is Creator *now*. Our scientific knowledge and technological expertise are subject to God's creative judgment through the responsibility God gave us to discover that all the forces of nature are links in the chain of love between God and the human family.

In silent contemplation after the reading, we join ourselves to creation in all its potential. Empty before God, we allow God to create us anew in this celebration. We may want to look at the paschal candle and allow Christ the redeemer to enlighten our minds with lively faith. Out of this depth we allow the Spirit to breathe where it wills. Together we cry out for global renewal in our response: "Lord, send out your Spirit, and renew the face of the earth." In the selections from Psalm 104 we shout our amazement and affirm God's wonderful deeds all over again.

The prayer is a further response. The presider, if he is perceptive, "collects" the sentiments of the community and voices them in the prayer. This prayer both expresses our realization of how God has gifted us as a community and voices a suitable petition. We ask that

we may perceive the "still more wonderful . . . new creation by which in the fullness of time you [God] redeemed your people [us] . . ." (*Sac.*, p. 188).

Second Reading: Genesis 22:1-18

Each successive reading is another stepping-stone on our
journey into full faith; each story reveals another facet
of our initiation into Christ. By the time we have come
this far on our journey, the elect surely are aware that
they are the new Isaacs, the uniquely beloved sons and
daughters of the Father in heaven and also of Mother
Church on earth. As the account of the sacrifice of Isaac
unfolds—now in view of the font and the altar—we
sense both type and antitype simultaneously, even as we
anticipate the wonderful multiplication of descendants
of Abraham that is taking place tonight.[35]

God has been revealing himself personally to humankind ever since human life began. This revelation has
engendered within the human community a dynamic
that we call *the promise*. The promise that we hear spoken
to Abraham is an inner vitality not unlike the assurance
imbedded within the kernel of an acorn: that it will grow
into a mighty oak tree. The growth is propelled from
within, and each stage of new life opens the way for
further promise. The story form—and Genesis 22 is a
masterpiece of storytelling—is preeminently suited to
sustain this inner dynamic, for when a story is well told,
it ends well because it "speaks of fundamental human
experience in such a way that it leads us back to that
experience to affirm it, to embrace it."[36]

The story of the sacrifice of Isaac unveils stages and
realms of meaning with which we in the twentieth century can identify. We find in it the source of our values,
and we reaffirm them. We need a firm sense of root-
edness on this night of family reunion. The Easter Vigil
presents an environment conducive to the joyful contemplation of "how we have grown!" We readily recognize Abraham as our "father in faith" and as the type

of our heavenly Father "who did not spare his own Son" (Rom. 8:32 NAB).

Even the manner in which the story marshals concepts and phrases helps us experience the depths of our connectedness. A case in point is the phrasing of the command: "Take your son Isaac, your only one, whom you love, and . . . offer him up as a holocaust. . . ." If we have been open to God's Word throughout Lent, our minds and hearts tend to connect these words with "Here is my servant whom I uphold, my chosen one with whom I am pleased" (Isa. 42:1 NAB), and again, with the Father's words at the baptism of Jesus, "This is my beloved Son. My favor rests on him" (Matt. 3:17 NAB). We turn our hearts to those who will become "offspring of Abraham" on this night. We sense with them the affirmation that these words offer. For six weeks they have been celebrating their privilege of being God's elect, God's chosen ones. All the sentiments evoked by the words of the story are part of the celebration, and thus part of the Spirit-sharing that the great Vigil is.

The fathers of the Church have viewed Isaac carrying the wood as a type of Jesus carrying his cross to Calvary. Isaac becomes a type of Jesus perhaps even more authentically when he elicits from Abraham the words "God himself will provide the sheep for the holocaust." Filled as we are with the readings of Lent and Triduum, our contemplation of these words could take us down different paths. On the one hand, we could enter into the Word of God that commanded the Jews to sacrifice a lamb, sprinkle their doorposts with its blood, eat the roasted lamb on the night they left Egypt, and then trace the course of the Passover (paschal) supper each year after they entered the promised land. Or our contemplation could take us by way of our growing insight into the meaning of salvation through a person. The seer who composed the song of the Suffering Servant that we proclaimed on Good Friday traveled this route "like a lamb led to the slaughter" (Isa. 53:7); and again: "If he gives his life as an offering for sin, he shall see his descendants in a long life" (53:10). Finally, if we move to John's word, "Look! There is the Lamb of God who takes away the sin of the world!" (John 1:29 NAB), the two paths converge in Jesus Christ, and the lamb becomes a person sent by God to free us to love.

Isaac speaks to our hearts as a type of the crucified and risen Lord in yet another way. Twice Isaac is rescued from death: first, God rescued him from the death of nonbeing by granting him life through the long-barren Sarah, and again God rescued him by reversing his command to Abraham to offer Isaac as a sacrifice. The new life of the risen Lord, the life that is growing within his Mystical Body, is symbolized in this scene. As these words are proclaimed in faith, the abundant power of the Spirit of Christ is released.

The risk that Abraham and Isaac took was very real, as was Jesus'. Those to be baptized know—even as do the faithful—that we must risk all. Psalm 16, our Responsorial Psalm, admirably expresses how hope exists within the eye of destruction and danger. "Keep me safe, O God; you are my hope." The message of this psalm spans the entire gamut of our life. Since the Lord is our "portion," we know intuitively in the depth of our being that we are meant for life everlasting. The psalm's final verse,

You will show me the path to life,
fullness of joys in your presence,
the delights at your right hand forever,

amply reveals that the fullness of relationship with God is total happiness. In his farewell address Jesus puts it this way: "Eternal life is this: to know you, the only true God, and him whom you have sent, Jesus Christ" (John 17:3 NAB).

The concluding prayer admirably synthesizes the dialogue that precedes it. In this prayer we recognize that God fulfills the promise to Abraham in the death and resurrection of Christ, when through the Paschal Sacraments God increases the chosen people throughout the world. This particular sequence of reading, response and prayer is one of the most strikingly clear examples of the living tradition of the Church of Christ. The promise of salvation proclaimed in the Abraham story has been fulfilled in Christ, and now, in the ministry of word and sacrament, it is applied to the community of faith.

Third Reading: Exodus 14:15-15:1

This scripture reading, which so vividly tells of the final tense moments before the Israelites crossed the Red Sea and of their joy afterwards could best be called the third stepping-stone of our faith journey that we celebrate in concentrated form on this night. In quiet expectancy we are praying our history as members of the family of God. At this point we allow ourselves to be present in faith to a key event of that history: the crossing of the Red Sea. As we contemplate this event in our celebration, we discover that we are releasing energies latent in the assembled community as well as those still hidden in the historical event. We are not simply looking at a picture and enjoying it. Rather, as we identify with this crisis event, we spark new insights in the same way a light flashes when two live wires touch.

The crossing of the Red Sea is a liminal or boundary experience. That is, the Israelites stand at an important choice-point. Although we have said that God always shapes the divine encounter with us according to our receptivity, that assertion does not indicate that in the encounter we—and, in the case of this reading, Israel— would not have to make a leap of faith to arrive at a place entirely different than our present one. On this night of decision, the elect are facing just that sort of faith leap; and every succeeding conversion calls us, the faithful, to this same leap of faith. The scripture story itself describes the final, tense moment before decisive action. A certain dynamism has built up within the Israelite community through the circumstances of the ten plagues, the eating of the Passover meal, and all else that went before. All these circumstances have come about under God's providence, and at this point the dynamism moves them toward action. Nevertheless, the people have to make their own free choice to act; God will not do it for them: "Why are you crying out to me? Tell the Israelites to go forward."

A similar dynamism has also been building up within the faith community, particularly since the beginning of Lent, and especially during the last few days of Triduum. We know that God is calling us to make a leap of faith. Instinctively we sense the danger inherent in such a move. Without a doubt, we too are risking everything to make the move symbolized by the act of crossing the waters. We have no assurance of the outcome except the promise of God, but of course that is the single unfailing assurance! The outstretched hand of Moses—the image is repeated four times in the passage—symbolizes the touch of divine concern.

The ambiguity of the water—saving some people and destroying others—is another symbolic reality. By juxtaposing these two opposite effects of the same water, God engenders a new hope in the hearts of the Israelites, a hope that enables them to say yes to the divine call. They come to know that the new identity they experience is that of being an entirely new people—God's holy people. Inasmuch as the Egyptians and their chariots and charioteers oppose Israel's becoming a free people, they symbolize whatever human persons need to relinquish each time they are called to a new stage of intimacy with God. On this night we, the Christian community, are enabled to identify with God's call and to make the radical choice it evokes.

Together, we also realize that when we proclaim these words on this night, Christ is present. In the light streaming from the Easter candle we recognize that the waters have been parted by the cross and resurrection. We have been moving around in darkness, with destructive forces in close pursuit. At this point in the celebration we already anticipate the Paschal Sacraments that will destroy our enemies (sin and death) and will call us more deeply into union as God's holy people. Like the Israelites, we look back and marvel at what might have been our fate. We also know that we have been saved, and like the Israelites we are unable to fathom how it all came about. For in our case also, it seems that God has done nothing but cast a glance at the hostile forces within us and "clogged their chariot wheels."

The response to this reading voices the sheer amazement of a new people conscious of the presence of the glory of the Lord. The Canticle of Moses from Exodus 15 expresses the courage that God has engendered within the hearts of the people. It also calls attention to the power of Pharaoh's army, the better to highlight the power of God's right hand. The canticle is the hero-worshipping of a newly formed people. As such, it is most appropriate on our lips this night when we too are so conscious of being God's people.

The prayer gathers up the amazement of God's people by admitting that "even today we see the wonders" (*Sac.*, p. 189) God worked so long ago. Furthermore, what God did by the power of his right hand[37] for a single people in delivering them from Egypt's slavery, God now offers to the whole world in our celebration of baptism, in which Jesus' passage from death to life unrestrictedly offers liberation and peoplehood to the entire human race. In the petition of the prayer we ask that all of us may acquire the privilege of new life. At one time this privilege was restricted to the children of Abraham and to the Israelites as a people. Now, through the waters of baptism, God extends the privilege to us all.

Fourth Reading: Isaiah 54:5-14

With Israel, we have made the radical choice that includes the risk of relinquishing any false security that has held us in bondage. Such a choice readies each of us for intimacy and develops our ability to respond in a committed way, that is, *as a person,* to the call of another person. This reading from Isaiah uses the love bond between husband and wife to reveal God's relation to his people. The image of husband and wife is one of the favorite images used by Israel to express its faith-response to God. By also employing the image of a well-guarded city, the reading mixes its metaphors, or at least uses them in close succession.

These two figures express a mutuality basic to humanity itself and thus to the faith community. God has both created and redeemed us. As creatures, we are part of the cosmos; as redeemed, we are within the stream of life known as salvation history. As creatures and as brides, we have been unfaithful and have roused God's anger. True, God is angry, because God cares; but by enduring love and compassion God transcends anger. Sin has its own punishment built into it. Sinners create for themselves their sense of being abandoned by God.

Earlier we saw how God planted the seed of hope directly in the paradise punishment of the Creation story as well as in the tragedy of Calvary. We find the same phenomenon in this reading. The reading compares the promise of hope to the oath God swore after the flood that the waters would never again deluge the earth. In this reading the firm foundation of the mountains and hills symbolizes God's unshakeable love. The language displays the tender, passionate superlatives characteristic of a lover's vocabulary: " . . . with great tenderness I will take you back; . . . with enduring love I take pity on you. . . . My love shall never leave you."

This reading also uses the city as a symbol of the broader social structure of God's people. That symbol leads us to recognize the power of the enemy that lays siege. We come o know that while the enemy is endangering our citadel, *God is building us up from within.* The inhabitants—ourselves—are being taught by God. In this night's celebration God establishes us "far from fear of oppression."

We cannot call attention often enough to our need to realize how essential it is for us to be in touch with the depths of our hearts, where alone we can *know* that God loves us passionately. When the reading touches that depth in us, the response rings true: "I will praise you, Lord, for you have rescued me" (Ps. 30:2). Through the verses chosen from Psalm 30 the Church expresses its joy at having been delivered from sorrow and destruction. Spontaneously our hearts will make connections: God's spousal love for us takes away our sorrow; and God's protection prevents our destruction. An infinite variety of nuances like the above exist, because members of the Body of Christ experience God's advances in their own unique ways, to the enrichment of the entire Body.

By broadening the promise made to Abraham to be the father of a great nation, God increases his own honor. In the prophetic words God reveals the depth of the divine relationship and also gives the people further assurances in which to trust. We are this people today, and we realize that God is still fulfilling the divine promise. In the petition of the prayer, we enter into the hope that God will bring that promise to even further completion in the Church on this holy night.

Fifth Reading: Isaiah 55:1-11

By reason of its depth of insight, this reading constitutes a high point of our celebration. The language is beautifully simple. We often express our deepest and most authentic longings in terms of basic human needs such as food and drink. Such symbolic language makes it possible for us to *know* with our entire being the meaning of God's invitation that rises in the depths of our hearts. We possess a kind of preconscious realization that *all is gift* and that on our own we are entirely unable to bring about our meeting with God. We can expend time, energy, and other resources, only to find that the things we have been seeking cannot satisfy. The invitation must come from God; and when it does, we realize that God gives the increase. New possibilities and new meanings arise, and we come to *know* the presence of God through them.

God's eternal covenant, like the promise made to Abraham, is ever being fulfilled. We need to hear this again and again. As a celebrating community, we hear it by attuning ourselves to nuances of language apt to strike sympathetic chords in us. The words "So shall you summon a nation you knew not" constitute one such phrase. In the context of the vigil celebration, it suggests how our encounter with God transforms us. Another such phrase is "the Holy One of Israel, who has glorified you." In scriptural language, this means that God gives a share in his dynamic love power. On this night, God's gift of power to David to witness God's covenantal love to the surrounding nations (Responsorial Psalm) becomes a symbol setting in motion the Christian's ability to witness to the transforming power of Christ.

Such a sublime dignity calls us to change our behavior, for it is all too possible to block God's action within us; we may miss the meaning of God's call, for, as the reading states, " . . . my thoughts are not your thoughts, nor are your ways my ways, says the Lord." Lucien Deiss says it well: "Dreams were sold, oracles bought, and gods tailored to man's measure. Israel knows only a transcendent God."[38]

The last two verses of this reading, "as . . . the rain and snow come down, . . . making it [the earth] fertile, . . . so shall my word be . . ." disclose again the power of God's Word. The evident yet surprising power of rain symbolizes the dynamism in the Word of God. Even watching rain fall upon the ground gives us a sense of how nature is gifted by and with a higher power to produce seed for the sower and bread for the eater. The rain does no violence, no manipulating. It simply and surely enables the grain to reach its goal, and that is all. Almost imperceptibly, this image leads us to ponder the word that goes forth from the mouth of God. It is a word of personal encounter; it does not constrain or violate human freedom. Yet it does assure us that we will arrive at the fullness God has promised. The proclamation of this word becomes a saving *event* for the faith community. Christ, the Word of God, has personally fulfilled God's promise and during our celebration is granting its fruition and increase by the power of the Holy Spirit.

The words of the Response give full and communal utterance to the yes of the celebrating community. Again we notice that the language of the Response does not simply provide a theological synthesis of the foregoing reading. Rather, it is a kind of "ruminating" or pondering over the insights the proclamation granted us. Subtle reminders of the foregoing reading do occur in the mention of such things as salvation, water, telling foreign nations (Isa. 12:2-6). All of these images tend to evoke renewed commitment and lead to the joyful imperative, "Shout with exultation, O city of Zion, for great in your midst is the Holy One of Israel!" The prayer that follows is quite general in tone. Still, it expresses two significant realities. It tells of the intimate, living connection between the words of the prophets and the mysteries being celebrated on this night. These latter are the acts God is currently performing. The prayer also recognizes that growth in goodness comes only by God's inspiration. In other words, the prayer helps us see that God is continuously breathing into us the breath of life through Christ, who in turn breathes his Spirit into us.

Sixth Reading: Baruch 3:9-15, 32; 4:4

As the Vigil progresses and the anticipation increases, the Word of God constantly leads us more deeply inward. Because it is proclaimed in the context of the Christian community as the community is in the process of celebrating the Paschal Sacrament,[39] the pericope from Baruch opens up even more clearly the spiritual insights of the Wisdom literature (written about 200 B.C.). In the setting of this night, in the twentieth century A.D., we hear Baruch's words in faith. They become for us an efficacious call once more. Furthermore, each member of the assembly will be moved in his or her own way according as the Spirit moves. A person may realize, for example, that he or she has been fettered by some bad habit and thus has "grown old in a foreign land." Another may experience a lack of peace, which indicates that his or her inner being wants to walk more fully "in the way of God." Still others may be moved by the Word to identify enough with the cosmos to say, "Here we are!" Even though we may each be moved by a different aspect of the Word of God, still, in the depths of our shared faith we become aware together that wisdom is indeed an inner law, for it is the living presence of God.[40] At this depth we can thrill together when we hear "Blessed are we, O Israel; for what pleases God is known to us!"

The Word of God moves us to sing our Response: "Lord, you have the words of everlasting life." These are words of Peter taken from John 6:69. The liturgy of this night constantly intertwines words from the New Testament with those of the Old. Such mingling is quite proper, for our heritage is a living one. The verses of Psalm 19 affirm that we will experience real peace when we heed the inner law of our hearts. Inner restlessness moves us to seek God ever more fully; and this searching, in turn, brings about growth in holiness.

The concluding prayer very simply sums up the fruits of contemplation. By addressing itself to the increase of the number of members in Christ's body, and by calling for God's continued care for those who are already members of the Body, the prayer also encapsulates the concerns of all who celebrate this night of vigil.

Seventh Reading: Ezekiel 36:16-28

The obvious contrast between the first and last part of this reading is truly an image of what God has been accomplishing within the Christian assembly celebrating on this night. The reading begins by painting a grim picture of Israel's sinfulness and punishment by exile. The second part of the reading, however, proclaims God's compassion in giving Israel a new heart. The Israelites have defiled their own land by sin and are spreading sin into the lands where they have been scattered. Still God does not destroy his people. Instead, God makes their sinfulness the occasion for more complete revelation of his unique holiness. God even gives the sinful people a fuller share in that holiness. The mystery that we share in the holiness of God by being gathered from foreign lands and being brought into their own land is being further accomplished here and now. The image "foreign lands" is appropriately symbolic of the disintegration we experience when we turn from our own best interests to sin. Those who have been "convicted of sin" by the Word of God have come this night to celebrate their conviction either by being baptized or by renewing their baptismal promises.

All are aware that their conversion is gift, i.e., that God acts "because of [his] holy name." Today God's assembled people are the beneficiaries of God's own holiness. Baptism fulfills the scriptural type as we are sprinkled with "clean water," and our being cleansed "from . . . idols" continues throughout life by the power of baptism.

The reading's promise of a new heart and a new spirit is very striking. God will restore to its rightful condition the natural human heart, which by sin became hard as stone; the new spirit to be given will be God's own life. This latter reality we can affirm and contemplate in faith; we can adore God and long for it; but only God can provide that gift in *God's* own time and manner. The prophetic references to water, to the spirit, and to the inner observance of God's law lead us to discover what our hearts really desire. Such stirring words inject new life into the celebrating community. When we hear the final verse, " . . . you shall be my people, and I will be your God," we know the joy of being the Church with the life-giving Spirit as our bond of unity.

The connection between this reading from Ezekiel and the sacrament of baptism is a dynamic one. It is not as if Ezekiel realized conceptually, i.e., saw in a vision, what the effects of baptism would be. Rather, as God's spokesman, the prophet makes a memorial of God's compassionate, never-ending love that by faith becomes present to us. In the Responsorial Psalm we call the desire of our hearts an inner thirst. The deer in its panting search for water becomes an apt symbol of our divinized human longing: "Like a deer that longs for running streams, my soul longs for you, my God." The remaining verses reveal to us, in metaphor, the object of our desire and direct us to recognize that God's power alone evokes this desire in us: "Send forth your light and your fidelity; they shall lead me on." The language is characteristic of lovers who savor the name of their beloved and do not hesitate to repeat it often:

> Then will I go in to the altar of God,
>   the God of my gladness and joy;
> Then will I give you thanks upon the harp,
>   O God, my God!

Although the concluding prayer contains no specific reference to the preceding reading, it does fulfill a function within the flow of the entire celebration. The vivid language employed in its original form adds much to its power. In the original Latin[41] this prayer addresses God as "unchanging power and everlasting light." It calls the Church a "wonderful sacrament" and refers to God as bringing about human salvation like one who quells (*tranquilator*) a storm.[42] Such concrete expressions not only add color; they also provide vivid metaphors to uncover meanings for a celebrating community in a manner that more abstract language cannot do. The prayer, then, clearly reveals Christ to be both the fulfillment of creation and the source of salvation—a revelation that is all-important during the Vigil.

The *Sacramentary* offers two optional prayers after the reading from Ezekiel. The first succinctly summarizes the relationship between the Old and the New Testament and contains a petition that grows out of the anticipation built up in our hearts by the opening proclamation. The second prayer—the one offered "if there are candidates to be baptized"—reveals a sense of anticipation and solicitude over the importance of our "ministry" in the sacramental action that is now so close (*Sac.*, p. 191).

Gloria and Opening Prayer

The singing of the *Gloria* at this point creates a certain ambiguity in the liturgy. Our experience of the continuity of salvation history might have been better served without this interruption. Ritually, however, it does heighten our anticipation as we near the first eucharistic celebration of the great Easter feast. The Opening Prayer expresses this sentiment well: "Lord God, you have brightened this night with the radiance of the risen Christ" (*Sac.*, p. 192). We are engaging in *the* celebration of our identity as "Church." Thus, when the prayer asks that the "spirit of sonship" be quickened in the Church, it broadens its application to include not only the initiation of new members through baptism but also the renewal of all the faithful.[43] The Vigil is not just a final instruction to those about to be baptized; the watch and prayer also prepare the faithful for intense participation in the celebration of the Paschal Sacraments.

Epistle: Romans 6:3-11

The risen Lord's radiance referred to in the Opening Prayer is not an empty figure of speech. The metaphor effectively puts us in touch with the divine-human power embodied in the proclamation of the selection from Paul's Letter to the Romans: "Are you not aware that we who were baptized into Christ Jesus were baptized into his death?" Inasmuch as these words are a living anamnesis or memorial of the experience that baptism has been for the faithful, they are words of celebration. At the same time they are *kerygma,* a kind of final call to those who are waiting for the celebration of their admission into union with Christ. In fact, the entire Christian community—particularly those of us who have been baptized as infants—stands in need of Paul's (the Church's) words. Much of the work of baptism needs still to be done. Hence we all need to hear the good news calling us to choose freely to let go of our sinful inclinations and to choose in faith to live by the selfless love of Christ crucified.

Paul's words then are not merely a commentary on the ritual action of baptism; still, they do seem to presuppose a ritual experience similar to that described by St. Cyril of Jerusalem in his *Mystagogical Catecheses.*[44] Being near to drowning is a basic human experience that can help us understand Paul's reference to our being buried with Christ in baptism. Cyril makes it clear that the *enemy,* not God's people, is destroyed there: "The tyrant of old was drowned in the sea; and this present one disappears in the salutary water."[45] Thus the adult catechumen, stripped naked, entering into a pool of water, and being submerged there receives firsthand experience of the destructive power "lurking" in the water. Being reminded of the proximate fear of drowning moves many persons to recognize the real danger that is sin, even as rising from the water heightens spiritual joy.

The vivid ritual action of baptism reveals, even makes present, the reality proclaimed in the selection from Romans. The experience of being buried in the water speaks loudly of our complete break with our sinful past, the break conversion implies. Conversion beckons us to salvation, but like all passage experiences, it is not without its dangers. Habits of behavior, attitudes of mind, and prejudices all die hard. Moreover, they often serve as masks and defense mechanisms. Therein lies a danger, for if we uproot defense mechanisms prematurely, before the new life has a firm foundation, we might destroy the first sprouts of new life and allow evil to triumph.

We need the full proclamation of God's Word, and we need its ritual enactment as well. Again and again we need to be affirmed in our faith-realization that our old self "was crucified with him" and that Christ's death "was death to sin, once for all." In ritual action, when we emerge from the water we make Christ's resurrection present, and we thrill that we are truly "alive for God in Christ Jesus." This Epistle is a clear example both of how the scriptural word reveals the meaning of a ritual action, and of how the ritual action releases the power in the Word of God.

Responsorial Psalm: Ps. 118:1-2, 16, 17, 22-23

Since, even at the heart of danger, God assures us of victory, we sing the Alleluia with full voice and "give thanks to the Lord, for he is good," not only in response to the reading from Romans, but in response to all that has gone on this night. No one but the Lord could transform the rejected stone into the cornerstone. Yet God is doing precisely that during our celebration.

Gospel: Matthew 28:1-10

Finally we arrive at the proclamation of the Gospel, the climax of the Liturgy of the Word. This story opens up to us even more of the meaning of our entire celebration. In proclaiming the resurrection, the fulfillment of all God's promises, the Gospel makes present the entire gamut of salvation history. It contains, in concentrated form, all the love advances God has ever made toward us. In this reading the Church witnesses to its identity as bride waiting and longing for the beloved. The Church knows that it subsists because of the dying and rising— the Easter passage—of Jesus.

Thus the Church lives in the constant watchfulness that this night of vigil symbolizes. The women in the gospel story who carry the aromatic spices and perfumed oil symbolize the Church motivated by the impulse of its heart. The Church—and we, the assembly, are the Church—awaits the dawn when it will encounter the risen Lord in the first Eucharist of Easter. Each year we make vigil, full of expectancy and longing. We, the baptized and the elect, hold ourselves ready to step across the boundary of our present condition and to follow the risen Lord. Even if some last-minute obstacles loom large, God does not disappoint our faithful waiting. For when we respond to the call to conversion, God, like the angel in the Gospel, removes all obstacles—all stones—from our path.

When the angel reveals the resurrection to the women, they are amazed.[46] The Church, too, has seen amazing resurrections throughout its history. Tonight the Church stands in the presence of all these resurrections and hails its glorified redeemer. Like the women at the tomb, the Church receives its mission anew as it stands in awe and wonder. "He [Jesus] has been raised, exactly as he promised. . . . go quickly and tell his disciples: '. . . [he] now goes ahead of you to Galilee, where you will see him.'" Like disciples, we will find the risen Lord in *our* "Galilees"—in the everyday places of our life.

Celebration of the Sacraments of Initiation

"The efficacy and the actuality of the living Word reach their *maximum* degree of realization on the further side of the proclamation itself, the sacramental action."[47] Those words sound like a theological reflection on the experience the paschal celebration has already begun to provide. We have been experiencing the real presence of Christ in the Liturgy of the Word, where we listened to the history of salvation unfold. We have also noted the gradual development of God's saving action during the forty days' journey to this holy night. The assembled community senses that it has arrived at another high point in celebration when it turns its attention toward the baptismal font.

Liturgy of Baptism

Godparents, catechists, sponsors, and others significant to the catechumens accompany the elect as they gather around the font. These people represent the community that will call forth new kinds of responses from the elect in the future. Those gathered around the font serve, for the entire community, as a symbol of the Church becoming the reality it is. This is an awesome moment. Its anticipation and expectancy are powerful assets for growth in relationships with God and with members of the Church as well. It is little wonder that the Church places the Litany of the Saints at this point. All members of the Church—the living and the dead—are engaged in interceding for the elect.

The fact that we bless the water does not indicate that it is unholy. In fact, by reflecting on water we discover some remarkable characteristics about it. Although it is colorless, shapeless, and flavorless, still it reflects all colors, adjusts to any shape, and is receptive of an infinite variety of tastes. It is the simplest everyday commodity, and yet it is absolutely indispensable for life. There is little wonder that it has become a universal archetype in the collective human unconsciousness.

We note that water has three powers, and all three enter into its symbolizing ability. First of all, water is a source of life and of the cosmos. No living thing could survive without it. A gentle rain gives new life to plants and animals. A glass of sparkling cool water quenches human thirst. Our pre-natal life in the amniotic fluid causes us to respond almost unconsciously to the importance of water. Water also has destructive power in floods that can devastate vast areas of life and property. It has the force to suck into its depths entire fleets during a storm at sea. It exerts its power to kill by drowning. Thirdly, and finally, its inherent ambiguity allows water to serve as a symbol of decision. Water's congenital power to bring opposites together makes it an appropriate vehicle for God to reveal his dealings with us. Our blessing of the water, then, is the Church's contemplation of water's varied symbolism put into words. Each wonderful deed mentioned in this prayer of blessing is like a flash of insight into one of the facets of the baptismal event, which is itself liberation and new life. The prayer of blessing ritually proclaims the series of wonderful deeds that reveal those aspects of the Christ Mystery that baptism celebrates. As we will see, the sacrament itself reveals the fuller meaning of that series of events.

The prayer states that our relation to God in Christ is an inner power. Baptism is not a kind of token gesture, a hurried in-the-water-out-of-the-water action that imprints an indelible mark on our souls. Rather, it is a decisive step on a long journey in faith. The awareness of the cosmic transcendent power that makes water the potential symbol of grace is a definite step toward deeper relationship with God. This awareness leads a person to discover the Holy Spirit breathing on the waters. The Spirit reveals God the Creator in the cosmos. The Spirit also reveals that when human beings become enslaved by too great an attachment to created things, they subject themselves to the destructive forces "lurking" in them. The story of the great flood reveals God as present in such a situation. In its contemplation, the Church discovers the waters of the deluge to be the symbol of the waters of baptism "that make an end of sin and a new beginning of goodness" (*Sac.*, p. 201).

After it mentions God in the cosmic forces, the prayer goes on to detail how the Church finds God in the account of salvation. The Red Sea becomes the site where water as a natural symbol becomes the sacrament of a human yes to God. Liberation requires an affirmation from those seeking to be freed. In any experience of conversion—including the one being celebrated this night—human persons must do just what God called the Israelites to do: give flesh to their yes to God. Only then they can advance, expecting God to create a path through the water. The prayer goes on to show that by his descent into the Jordan, Jesus was anticipating his final victory over the demonic powers that lurk within the cosmos as the result of sin. He was baptized in the baptism of repentance. Since Jesus came as a representative of the entire human race, his baptism included our yes to God as well as his own. God reveals the Trinity through the voice of the Father and the appearance of the Spirit in the form of a dove over Jesus, the Son, not only to those gathered at the Jordan but to all who gather at the baptismal font.

The most complete yes of humankind, the one that is the source of every sacrament, was spoken by Jesus on the cross as he willed blood and water to flow from his side.[48] Several of the fathers of the Church speak of this phenomenon as the sacrament of the whole Church. By its power, Jesus could send the apostles into the world to baptize in the name of the Trinity. "But what makes of the baptismal water the assured vehicle of grace is the very Word of God in Jesus Christ and it alone: 'Go, teach ye all nations and baptize them in the name of the Father and of the Son and of the Holy Ghost.'"[49] The effect of this sending extends into our own time.

All relationship with God is the work of the Holy Spirit. The Church liturgically expresses this understanding in the form of an epiclesis, and this blessing prayer proves no exception. Once again, however, the petition form of the epiclesis should not be interpreted as indicating the Spirit's prior absence. Rather, the epiclesis ritually expresses our willingness to enter into the action of the Spirit and into the mystery of Christ to be effected in us once again. Only by the power of the Spirit can water become salvific and become the vehicle of union with God. Since the fall of humanity, no created matter is ever neutral. Because of the way human beings use it, created matter can be either an instrument of human sinfulness—as money is to so many people today—or the carrier of divine life. The prayer for the blessing of water in the Byzantine rite says this well:

But do Thou, O Master of all, show this water to be the water of redemption, the water of sanctification, the purification of the flesh and spirit, the loosing of bonds, the remission of sins, the illumination of the soul, the laver of regeneration, the renewal of the Spirit, the gift of adoption to sonship, the garment of incorruption, the fountain of life.[50]

Thus the natural power of water is not lost. Matter is maintained as good; in fact, water reaches its highest goodness when it becomes a symbol that brings human beings into the reality made present in the prayer of "blessing." Such is the height for which this colorless, flavorless, shapeless, limpid mass is destined.

Finally the longed-for moment arrives. Waiting has a value for spirituality, because the intensity of the longing serves to create openness to accept the good we long for. Even impatience for deliverance can be valuable: "Indeed, the whole created world eagerly awaits the revelation of the sons of God" (Rom. 8:19 NAB). At least three times during the catechumens' period of preparation, the celebrating assembly prayed in the Scrutinies to support them in their struggle against the forces of the evil one. Now it is time for the elect, freely and in faith, to renounce Satan, his works, and his empty promises. As adults they must finally speak for themselves. They do this in response to the threefold questioning by the president of the assembly.

By renouncing Satan, the elect open up a chasm, for they publicly let go of any securities and/or attachments to their former way of life, even though they have no foothold as yet on the new path. The elect really are like the Israelites when the waves of the Red Sea parted and Moses ordered them to cross over. By relinquishing their old, false securities they find themselves in the interval between death and resurrection. At this juncture they discard their clothing and are anointed with the oil of the catechumens. Strategically placed in the gap between the old and the new life, this anointing becomes the symbol of encouragement in the dark valley. Being rubbed with oil anticipates the victory over the evil one, which every act of conversion is. After any person's decision to change, a hiatus of doubt follows. "Can I do it? Will I do it? Do I really want to do it?" This empty space is a moment of dense darkness and danger.[51] But when we remember it after the victory, it adds zest to our rejoicing. The faithful who share the celebration thrill anew at their own deliverance as well, and their joy adds a current of hope to the environment.

Nudity is also an important symbol, and we need to say a word about it. Liturgically, it harkens back to the message of the reading from Genesis on the First Sunday of Lent. Thus it is related to the entire season of preparation as a global symbol of sin and the confusion it brings; for now it is not an expression of original innocence but of confusion and an exaggerated sense of charm. As such, it powerfully conveys the disorder that sin has brought to humankind. In the face of this helplessness, the longing for a personal savior is intensified.

In the early Church the triple profession of faith in the Trinity was made while the elect were in the water. It was accompanied by a triple submersion into the water by the hand of the bishop. Being submerged by a hand not one's own, and arising in the name of the Father and of the Son and of the Holy Spirit made this a uniquely significant symbol to break open the meaning of the bath and to reveal it as a "mystical sharing in the death and rising of Christ, by which believers in his name die to sin and rise to eternal life" (RCIA #32). However, the present formula, "I baptize you in the name of the Father, and of the Son, and of the Holy Spirit" (RCIA #220), tends to tone down the impact of the contrast between death and resurrection.

All along the journey leading up to this moment, God has offered us intuitions that God is a personal God. At the moment of the elect's death and rising in baptism, God is revealed as such through the words used by the minister of the sacrament. The resurrection of those baptized in Christ becomes their entry into the very life of the Trinity. They experience a new source of motivation, and they *know* that the words of Paul about dying and rising, heard earlier in the Epistle, have now been actualized.

The new life has begun, conversion will continue, and the otherness of that new way of life will keep on moving. The clothing with the white garment can be a powerful, albeit secondary, symbol. It symbolizes putting on Christ and the Christian world-view as a way of life. Creation, fall, redemption, world economy, race relations, social justice—all these are part of true Christian life. For when a human person has been regenerated in communion with others, he or she becomes personally committed to assume more fully the responsibility to "rule the earth" (Gen. 1:28). The white garment becomes the "robe of glory" meant to help the neophytes keep the Christian meaning of human life actively before their minds and hearts. Similarly, the lighted candle symbolizes the light of faith that, unlike a fire that can be either destructive or creative, does not destroy any of God's creations but only reveals them in the light of faith. Thus Christian life is truly incarnational. It is not "primarily a moral concept, but an ontological reality; the divine reality; the divine reality communicating his [God's] intimate and proper life to some of his children."[52]

Liturgy of Confirmation

There is a sense in which we might say that, in the Western church at least, the sacrament of confirmation is a sacrament "seeking a theology." As it now stands, the *Rite of Christian Initiation of Adults* places confirmation immediately after baptism.

After calling on the Holy Spirit as the sevenfold Gift of the Father, the president of the assembly lays hands on and anoints the neophytes with perfumed oil.[53] The words "be sealed with the Gift of the Holy Spirit" (RCIA #231) reveal the meaning of this gesture and make it abundantly clear that the Holy Spirit is the proto-symbolizer who directs the entire process of initiation. Confirmation, then, which has come to be regarded as a sacrament in its own right, could well be seen as the epiclesis par excellence of the Paschal Sacraments.[54] Even though both the blessing of the baptismal water and the Eucharistic Prayer have their own epiclesis, the sacrament of confirmation stands between them as the sign that the Spirit is given to those who are initiated in the complex but single process of the *Rite of Christian Initiation of Adults*.

The anointing with chrism is an appropriate symbol of our special *character* as Christians. On this night of vigil, the anointing celebrates the presence of the Holy Spirit—the Spirit of Christ—within the community's memory. This entire Vigil is a memorial during which the Spirit of Jesus progressively inserts the community of believers into the Easter passage, the dying and rising of Jesus.

Liturgy of the Eucharist

Having been sealed as members of the celebrating assembly, the newly baptized are ready to be admitted to the "family table" of the eucharistic celebration. Moreover, although the faithful renew their own experience of baptism and confirmation as they participate in the initiation of the neophytes, it is important to make their renewal explicit. Our lenten observance has been directed to this occasion. We, the faithful, publicly reaffirm our renunciation of Satan and sin, and in the Profession of Faith we renew our entry into the life of the Blessed Trinity, the life of the Church. The important tactile experience of being sprinkled with Easter water helps us experience our involvement in the Easter passage, our new passage from death to life. This renewal of the faithful serves liturgically to express our identification with the newly initiated.

As we approach the holy table with the neophytes among us for the first time, we delight in the special features of our shared identity. Together we speak freely to God in faith and approach God in confidence (Eph. 3:12). This celebration of Eucharist and sharing of Communion is the climax, the zenith toward which the neophytes, and the faithful along with them, have been journeying since the First Sunday of Lent—actually, since the neophytes first heard the good news. To understand the importance of this moment, we will discuss the sacrament of the Eucharist under four headings: (1) the overall human symbolism inherent in meals; (2) the *berakah*, the prayer that reveals the meaning of the Old Covenant, particularly as celebrated in the annual Passover meal; (3) the Eucharistic Prayer, which reveals the meaning of the eucharistic meal of the New Covenant; (4) the sharing of the sacramental food and drink of the meal in the context of this night's initiatory event.

1. *Symbolism of Meals.* Meals possess an evocative power that is deeply imbedded in human consciousness. An active awareness of what meals mean to us helps us better understand the eucharistic meal as the summit of initiation.

The most obvious reality about meals is that they are food and drink. Meals furnish the necessary fuel for life. But food and drink mean more to us than physical sustenance. We humans tend to "humanize" our food. Even the way we prepare our meats, vegetables, and drinks indicates that food has deeper meaning, that it points to something beyond itself. Our bread and wine are both the "fruit of the earth and the work of human hands" (*Sac.*, p. 371). Somehow the crushing of the grains of wheat and the grapes and the ensuing "human" processes necessary for their preparation captures our imagination and says something about solidarity and effort.

Furthermore, the meals themselves possess a social character. They provide not only the environment in which our physical life is maintained but also provide the social bonding and security necessary for human development. On a deeper level, meals express friendship. We do not say, "Come to my house for dinner," or "Let's have lunch together sometime," to just anyone. We extend such invitations to special persons, persons to whom we are committed. The food we share engenders even further commitment. Meals, therefore, both express and intensify social unity. In fact, meals do this so well that we usually celebrate such significant occasions as birthdays, anniversaries, and weddings with meals.

Besides the physical and the social, meals *can* have a specifically religious dimension.[55] The outstanding Old Testament meal, the one that possesses all the steps of revelation of meaning, is the one eaten just before God's people left Egypt.[56] The Israelites certainly needed nourishment that night, for they had no idea when they would eat again. In addition, they needed strong social bonds to get out of Egypt together. Finally, they needed an overarching and shared religious meaning for what they were about to do together. The meal provided that meaning. And that meaning was covenantal faith. Thus faith transformed still further the already symbolic meal. The meal revealed to the Israelites that they could trust God's power and will to save them. They professed this faith when they sprinkled the blood of the lamb on their doorposts. The moment they performed this symbolic, faith-filled gesture they were already saved spiritually from the shackles of Egypt's slavery. But their liberation had still to be carried out physically, externally. The Passover meal not only provided physical nourishment and social bonding, it also became the symbol of God's sustaining power until the Israelites found themselves safe on the other side of the Red Sea. In this way the food and the social bonding achieved their highest meaning for the Israelites as sources and expressions of a new and deeper relationship with God and with one another in faith and love.

The New Testament meal, the Last Supper, also possesses all the elements described in the Passover meal. In fact, it contains ritual elements that celebrate the entire sweep of salvation history, both in the Old and the New Testaments. At this meal, when Jesus reveals that in his Passion and death he becomes food to be eaten and drink to be imbibed, the basic meanings of food as human *nourishment,* as social *bonding,* and as the *celebration of covenant* between God and the chosen people are superseded. Jesus seals an even closer social bond at this meal—the faith/spiritual bond—in his own blood. Like the Passover meal, the Last Supper also demands continued and future trust—not the trust to pass over the Red Sea, but the trust to pass over the chasm of death; for Jesus' "failure" on the cross would radically test the disciples' faith. Finally—again like the command of the Passover meal—this *new* Passover supper calls God's people to accept Jesus' command of faith and to display it in ritual action in the future: "Do this as a memorial of me."

2. *The Berakah.* Our Jewish ancestors developed a form of prayer that aids us in our search for the meaning in meals. The prayer is known as the *berakah.* Louis Bouyer states that this form of prayer "is the response which finally emerges [in Judaism] as the preeminent response to the Word of God."[57] Since the Word of God reveals the meaning of God's action on behalf of his people, the *berakah* is never merely abstract. It is a prayer of praise that always refers to one or more of the wonderful deeds through which God fulfills his promises.

The *berakah* begins with a laudatory address to God. It includes more, however, than simply thanking God for some favor. Since it involves a relationship, the prayer response, made in faith, proceeds from within the mystery of our having been gifted. In other words, when we pray the prayer, we not only recall and tell the story of how God has gifted us, we actually make memorial of the encounter with God and make it present. Thus our praise and thanks rest upon the *present* reality of an encounter with God. Petition is the third element of the *berakah* prayer, and it flows from the first two. When we praise God for past favors, we implicitly express our willingness to enter more fully into God's plan in the future. Thus petition or intercession follows as a matter of course. Finally, the prayer closes with another expression of praise known as a doxology.[58]

During the Passover meal this form of prayer was prominent. The annual celebration of the Passover was—and remains today—the occasion to retell the entire (Hebrew Testament) story of God's bounty and encounter with the Israelites. The celebration of the Passover meal also reaffirms the grand sweep of wonderful deeds that God performed on behalf of the chosen people. Jews recognized God's presence at the Passover meal, and there, through ritual that included the *berakah* prayer, they re-dedicate and recommit themselves to the covenant of God's love. The sentiments to which the *berakah* prayer form gives utterance are universally human as well as Jewish. Any human community that allows God to be God in its life can respond to the great movements found in this prayer form.

3. The Eucharistic Prayer. If there is ever a time when the Eucharistic Prayer finds its full significance, it is on this holy night when neophytes and the rest of the faithful have reached the climax of the initiation/renewal event. It expresses sentiments that have been evoked during the entire Vigil. Our treatment of the Eucharistic Prayer may seem a bit technical, but it is important to make every effort to discover the full living value beneath the words of this prayer we hear so often. The *General Instruction of the Roman Missal* of 1969[59] lists the chief elements of the prayer: (a) thanksgiving, (b) acclamation, (c) epiclesis, (d) narrative of the institution and consecration, (e) anamnesis, (f) offering, (g) intercession, (h) final doxology. We will see how these are an expansion of the Jewish *berakah* prayer model.

On this night we have feasted on the extraordinarily rich fare of God's Word. Now we approach the table of the sacrament, which in its turn becomes the "sign of a people who live amazed at the God who has shown himself to us in Jesus and amazed at the vision of human life and destiny which he has opened up."[60] This symbolism helps us recognize that our perception is not in our minds only, but that our thanksgiving brings about a *real* event.[61]

We are introduced into the great prayer only gradually, and God is always the inviting presence. In the Prayer over the Gifts—and this prayer always stands looking both to the presentation of the gifts and to their meaning as revealed in the Eucharistic Prayer—the president of the assembly quite simply affirms that the sacrifice we are offering is *our* liturgical celebration *today*. *We* are in the midst of the celebration by which the Church is reborn and nourished (*Sac.*, #206).

The introductory dialogue of the Preface follows. Since this dialogue is acclamatory, it affects the entire assembly. Like other acclamations such as slogans and yells, it has power to help us recognize our common sentiment and be conscious of our mutual commitment. In this dialogue, the natural vitality engendered in the back-and-forth movement between priest/presider and assembly becomes a vehicle of transcendence and a symbol of the first order. During the sacred action of the liturgy, the give-and-take of the dialogue reveals that the *meaning* of the intercommunication inherent in human existence is the continuing dialogue between God and his people.[62] When the interchanges of the dialogue are lively and actually stir up a response from those dialoguing, and when they come from hearts filled with faith, their power will be released in a way that truly corresponds with the sign (L. #7).[63]

On this night *in particular* the Christian community has its heart lifted up to the Lord in mutual commitment, it is now, immediately after the celebration of baptism and confirmation and/or their renewal. The encounter with the Lord that has taken place just moments before influences both priest/presider and the remainder of the assembly. They could at this moment be compared to open radars oriented by their relation to each other.[64] Given such openness, the actual words of a dialogue become less important than the context and mood in which they are spoken. This is certainly the case on this evening, for not only have we arrived at the high point of *this* celebration, but this celebration itself is the summation of all that has gone before, from pre-catechumenate through Lent and especially through the Sacred Triduum.

The Preface is an integral part of the Eucharistic Prayer. It does more than provide a verbal link with the preceding dialogue. It is more than an introduction, too, for it gives utterance to who we are and what we are about. When we identify God as Father, we also identify ourselves. Both our act of praise and thanks and our Christian identity proceed "through Christ our Lord." We give thanks, for all of this is gift indeed! Still, we are not simply glad over an acquisition of some kind. Rather, the gift is an interior one, and we have come to recognize a new depth of relationship with God. We speak our praise and thanks when we publicly *acknowledge* what is transpiring. Who can fathom the depth of the "riches and the wisdom and the knowledge of God"? (Rom. 11:33 NAB) Ledogar's perceptive work on early Greek praise verbs gives us an insight into the profound meaning imbedded in what we translate as "thanksgiving and praise."[65] These verbs indicate in the Greek that those who use them recognize their relationship to God and accept its consequences.

Imagine the impact these words make on the neophytes who hear them for the first time. They recognize that "Eucharist—thanksgiving and praise—is the very form and content of the new life that God granted [us] when in Christ he reconciled [us] with himself."[66] When, for that matter, any of us—whether in a communal celebration or in contemplation alone—recognizes that God has compassionately expiated our sins and made us his children, assurance of new life invades us. We recognize that our identity transcends our citizenship, our family ties, and even our psychological health. Such self-identity includes an awareness of our vital interrelatedness with all the other members of the Mystical Body. We can never fabricate who we are. It is always *gift!* It is little wonder, then, that in the early centuries only those who had been initiated by baptism and confirmation were allowed to be present when the Eucharist was celebrated.

"We do well, always and everywhere" (*Sac.*, p. 415). Although these words are a very "flat" translation of the stronger *"Dignum et justum est,"* they still give us pause. They help us know who we are, help us *acknowledge* our identity, and help us act in harmony with it. When we pray these words, we are becoming who we are as God's children. This is the acme of integration; this is human personhood at its best. On this night of nights we can fully understand the words of Scripture: "And God saw that it was good" (Gen. 1).

In our treatment of the *berakah* we saw that the acknowledgment of praise and thanks on the part of a worshiping community rests upon its *present* awareness of having been gifted by God. At this point in our celebration of the Vigil we are at the height of such awareness. The entire history of salvation that we heard in the proclamation of God's Word has climaxed in the proclamation of the resurrection. We have already entered into the Paschal Mystery in the sacraments of baptism and confirmation. The Preface artistically expresses these communal experiences in order to convey our here-and-now acknowledgment of God in his gifting. Our praise and thanks, then, encompass all of God's compassionate transformation of the human community by the divine presence within it.

We praise you with greater joy than ever
    on this Easter night,
when Christ became our paschal sacrifice.
He is the true Lamb who took away the sins of the
    world.

By dying he destroyed our death;
by rising he restored our life. (*Sac.*, p. 415)

The Preface's construction serves to enhance the prayer's meaning. At this moment our praise and thanks acknowledges that "we have been there" and that we *know* that Jesus' full submission to the Father has become the sacramental power breaking the death-grip sin has had on us. In his resurrection, of course, Jesus did more than restore our human life to its original state. He regenerated us by his resurrection;[67] that is, he gifted us with a *new* ability to respond affirmatively in faith to the Father *now* during our mortal life. Neophytes and the rest of the faithful can truly say, "We have been there!" when they hear these words of the Preface.

In that happy frame of mind, we move to reflect on the Narrative of the Institution and Consecration.[68] This is the story par excellence that has been revealing the meaning of Christian life for centuries. As a story, it takes us again through the paces of Jesus' complete self-gift and calls us to follow him. It begins by mentioning a certain historical time and set of circumstance to help us recall that what we are doing is rooted in historical events and not in cosmic myth.

When Jesus took the bread and "said the blessing" *(benedixit)*, he knew—and his disciples knew—that he was entering into the ancient ritual action that his ancestors had celebrated for centuries as a memorial of God's encounter with them.[69] As "he said the blessing," Jesus entered into the collective memory of his people and made present God's encounter with them. Jesus used the historical sequence of events[70] to reveal a present divine encounter, as did every head of a Jewish family during a Passover meal.[71] Above all else, Jesus *knew* that he was himself the fulfillment of all of these events. What a wealth of overtones the phrase "he said the blessing" has for us on this night, especially when we realize that we have memorialized God's encounter in the sequence of Scripture passages proclaimed in the light streaming from the Easter candle!

Our eucharistic meal becomes a "new" encounter with God as we perform the sacred liturgical action.[72] The words of Jesus in the Narrative give us the meaning of our action. The action is *now*. The proclamation is being made at this time in *our* history, and it is made ritually; it is *our* act of acknowledging and breaking forth in praise and thanks for God's merciful presence. Thus the entire assembly—all of us—is *now* engaged in the presence of the bread and the cup. In his words of Institution and Consecration, Jesus again makes present his saving action in us.

In the context of our present celebration, Jesus' words disclose a vision of transcendent human possibility. This symbolic/sacramental action beckons all who participate in it to enter into that transcendence. The very ambiguity of the symbols—the bread broken and shared, and the cup of the covenant passed around and shared—adds power to move hearts. We discover new meaning for our lives when we see the whole cruel execution on Calvary disclosed as the epitome of God's merciful compassion and of humanity's acceptance of it. The broken body and spilled blood that speak of human brokenness and failure also speak of nurture: "This is my body, which is for you." The unjust execution means new bonding, "This cup is the new covenant in my blood" (1 Cor. 11:25 NAB). What once looked like the shattering of all human hopes becomes the holiest and most salutary of actions. The chief symbols characteristically used by human beings to express and to seek union with God—sharing a meal and sealing a covenant—are revealed as being the *person* of Jesus in his action of dying and rising. The meaning of our lives as being part of that same passover from death in sin to newness of life in Christ is thus effected. The words of Jesus, "Do this in memory of me" (*Sac.*, p. 549), bring our realization of his active presence among us to the point of ecstasy—out of ourselves and into him. We recognize the meaning of our action as a call to the messianic banquet.

To the degree that we as a worshiping assembly are involved in the meaning of this sacred action, our memorial acclamation will be spontaneous—a kind of "standing ovation." Of all the four alternative responses, the first, the simple staccato "Christ has died, Christ is risen, Christ will come again" (*Sac.*, p. 550) seems to be most appropriate applause at the moment of memorial. The body of the faithful recognizes the risen Christ among us *now* and shouts out its awareness that this liturgical mystery does indeed embody the past, the present, and the future.

All that has been proclaimed in the Eucharistic Prayer thus far has truly been made present. Still, the prayer adds even further ritual clarification in its recollection of Christ's death and resurrection and our anticipation of his return. The anamnesis (as the above-mentioned recollection is named) picks up and explicitly expresses what the assembly has just proclaimed intuitively. Such recognition of Christ's saving activity, along with the words of offering that usually accompany it, is another yes to the God who calls us to plunge into an unknown future of growth. It is one more acceptance of the challenge: "Your attitude must be that of Christ" (Phil. 2:5 NAB).

The entire Eucharistic Prayer, which tells us the meaning of what we are doing, is spoken in the power of the Holy Spirit. If ever the Spirit "signals God's wedded presence to and within human life and activity,"[73] it is on this holy night at the climax of the celebration of the Paschal Sacraments. In the sacrament of confirmation we have just celebrated the presence of the Holy Spirit. Consequently we do not doubt that the Spirit is here. So our epiclesis (the name given to the invocation of the Holy Spirit) is simply our overt response—a kind of "yes, please"—to what we know will be the Spirit's effect upon the twofold action of the sacred meal. Like any other meal, this sacramental banquet offers both nourishment and social bonding. If we wish to discover God's meaning in Holy Communion, we need to recognize how the Spirit acts on both.

In light of what we have seen about the meaning of the bread and wine in our reflections on the Institution Narrative, we realize that much more than a change of one substance to another is at stake here. Thus when we pray, in the pre-Narrative epiclesis, "Let your Spirit come upon these gifts . . . so that they may become for us the body and blood of our Lord, Jesus Christ" (Eucharistic Prayer II, *Sac.*, p. 549), we are doing more than calling upon God's substance-changing power. We are opening ourselves to the energies of the Spirit's powerful presence. This prayer describes the action by which God's Spirit provides us with the true nourishment for our spirits. In its earliest form, the Eucharistic Prayer of St. Basil seems to express this action of the Spirit quite well. Using the verb *ánadeíknûmi* ("to reveal what was hidden"), the prayer asks God, " . . . send your Holy Spirit upon us and upon these gifts . . . to reveal to us this bread in very truth as the precious body of . . . Jesus Christ, and this chalice as in very truth the precious blood of our Lord and Savior Jesus Christ."[74]

The eucharistic meal also effects social bonding. In the invocation that, in the Roman rite, we make after the Narrative, we ask that we may be able to respond to the Spirit's action uniting us as members of the Body of Christ. This transcendent social goal is very much a part of the total celebration of this night, the night on which we have been so concerned with the increase of God's family through the sacraments of initiation.

The intercessions follow the epiclesis. Schmemann calls intercession an absolutely essential act: "To be in Christ means to be like Him, to make ours the very movement of his life. And as He 'ever liveth to make intercession' for all 'that come unto God by him' (Heb 7:25), so we cannot help accepting his intercession as our own."[75] In the intercessions we say, in effect: "Yes, we want you to be to us, O God, who you truly are. We have acknowledged you in praise and thanksgiving by telling the story of your wonderful deeds."

Once we have caught the meaning of what has been happening thus far in our celebration, and once we have followed the impulse toward commitment inherent in the Eucharistic Prayer, we are bound to recognize how needy we are. We long for more intimate relationship with the Father in the bond of the Mystical Body of Christ. Therefore we include intercessions for persons who have key enabling roles in the Body; and as we do so, we become ever more aware of the growing Kingdom and of our role with Christ to make intercession, just as Christ does at the right hand of the Father. As we carry the joyful awareness of the presence we are celebrating in the Eucharist, and as our care and concern for others increases, our intercessions will become both more universal and more specifically connected with the Kingdom.

The Eucharistic Prayer's final act of praise, the doxology, gives climactic utterance to our awe and admiration. On this night as we gather around the table of the Lord we are keenly aware of our identity. We acknowledge the meaning God gives to this food and drink. The transcendent meaning of this food has been revealed already in the course of the entire celebration and most specifically in the Narrative of the Institution and Consecration. We are clearly at a point where we can recognize that the words proclaimed earlier (see Isa. 55:1-11) have truly been creative. God's Word is not returning void but is "achieving [now] the end for which [he] sent it." The praise and thanks flowing from our hearts is more than the perception of our minds. It is an *event*. Elevating the mystery-bearing bread and wine could be likened to proposing a toast in God's honor. We are at a memorial banquet in which Christ Jesus is our praise and also our food.

The doxology contains in concentrated form all that has preceded it. It clearly expresses the mediatorship of Christ, and it directs all to the Father in the unifying and pervading action of the Holy Spirit. It recapitulates the entire prayer by bringing together its key movements in a compact, contemplative, and poetic form. Inasmuch as it is addressed to the Father, it reiterates the laudatory address. Since the prepositions of the doxology indicate relatedness, a look at them reveals something of the breadth and depth of our union with Christ. Our bodiliness is caught up into Christ incarnate as we praise the Father *through* him. Our peer relationship, which the Father's freely offered adoption has established, and in which we have been enabled to communicate with God, is expressed by our praise *with* Christ. Finally, since we have been given the Spirit of love, we praise God *in* Christ, knowing that he is the lover who holds us in his heart. This threefold expression of relationship with Christ is a contemplative utterance, not a search for reasoned theological statement.

It is also very important not to transport the phrase "in the unity of the Holy Spirit" (*Sac.*, p. 551) into the ineffable realms of the Blessed Trinity, as it were. The phrase is epicletic; that is, it expresses the Spirit's presence among us, and hence it belongs very much on earth. We are the Church, the Body of Christ. We are alive as a Body in the unity being wrought by the Holy Spirit here and now. The preposition *of* here translates a subjective genitive and denotes *authorship*. Paraphrased, it would read: "in the unity which the Holy Spirit is here and now forming."[76]

The phrase "all honor and glory is yours" (*Sac.*, p. 551) is a clear indication that *acknowledgment* is the bottom line of right relationship with God. We are human beings who are expressing our relationship with God, and honor and glory plays an important part in it. Conceptually, the two words mean the same thing. The singular verb both in Latin and (fortunately) in English seems to indicate that Christians recognize this. The term *glory* was used in early Christian texts to mean the divine power and otherness of God. Their use of *glory* to mean also that share in divine life that God grants us in Christ demonstrates how the early Christians experienced their relationship to God. Irenaeus says, "The glory of God is man fully alive."

Like that of our forebears, our personal potential reaches its highest mark when the human community accepts divine love into its life and affirms all the merciful, personal gifts of salvation history. These gifts—each of them a call to new depths of relatedness—have again been granted during the sacred action of our liturgical celebration. They have been entirely gratuitous, and yet in a real sense they have been elicited within the living body of the assembly. Therefore, the phrase "all honor and glory is yours" gathers into one harmony the multifaceted anamnesis (memorial) of God's wonderful deeds. Such glory, since it is God's transcendence immanent in the human community, belongs to God *in the Church*. In short, the doxology is one grand call to affirm our identity and our actions *as Church*.

The entire Eucharistic Prayer is a call for an affirmative response, a commitment, from those celebrating. That is the natural internal atmosphere of a meal also. The mounting crescendo of praise that reaches ecstasy level in the doxology releases a volume of psychic and spiritual energy that breaks out in the "Amen." This "Amen" gives us pause. "It is commitment, vulnerability, and a willingness to let something happen."[77] Specifically, at the end of the Eucharistic Prayer we are surrendering ourselves to the frame of mind that is proper at any meal and, in this case, proper to the mind of Christ Jesus. In some ways this "Amen" is the most important word of the entire prayer, if not of our entire lives.

4. *The Eucharistic Meal in the Context of This Night.* Finally we are ready to approach the table of the Lord and share the food and drink he has prepared for us. We have celebrated the memorial of God's benevolence already in the rich fare of the table of the Word on this night; we have entered into the death and rising of Jesus Christ in the sacrament of baptism; in the sacrament of

confirmation we have received the Spirit; and we have also celebrated our response to what is explicitly happening in the Eucharistic Prayer. As a people we are in the midst of celebrating all that the Paschal Mystery has ever entailed; the divine benevolence has been rendered present, and now we are nourished with it in the meal. Rouillard evidences the growing awareness abroad today—awareness of the close bond between the Liturgy of the Word and the Liturgy of the Sacrament when he says, "The liturgy of the word elicits the liturgy of the meal, which now actualizes the past event."[78] The Lord's Prayer is an appropriate table prayer, for it contains and expresses the epitome of God's work of salvation.

The gestures of breaking the one bread and of dividing the one cup are very important. These actions flow from our realization of Christ's action on our behalf, and of the broken character of the Body of Christ; they also form a link with the Eucharistic Prayer that gives us the meaning of the action. The sacred meal that celebrates our sharing in the Paschal Mystery and our bonding in the Body of Christ is effected in our apparently ordinary action of eating and drinking. It is "eucharistized" food and drink that we receive. Thus praise, remembrance or memorial, invoking of the Holy Spirit, and intercessions are all reaffirmed when we partake of the bread and the cup. This is *not* an individual tête-à-tête with Jesus. "In the Eucharist we . . . are swept up into the loving energies of Jesus for one another, for his whole body."[79]

This sacred banquet culminates our entire celebration. We began by bringing the entire cosmos into our celebration in the experience of changing darkness into light. The Liturgy of the Word then brings all of salvation history into this moment of fulfillment. Finally, when the newly formed family of God—neophytes and faithful—shares in food and drink around our Father's table, we crown the sacraments of initiation.

After sharing the sacred meal, we close with a very brief prayer: "Lord, you have nourished us with your

Easter sacraments" (*Sac.*, p. 206). (The term Easter Sacraments, *sacramenta paschalia*, in this context means all the words, gestures, and other symbols that have been part of our celebration.) Therefore, "Fill us with your Spirit, and make us one in peace and love. We ask this through Christ our Lord" (*Sac.*, p. 206). Finally, our joy explodes: "The Mass is ended, go in peace, alleluia, alleluia." Our Easter passage has spelled another victory for our risen Lord! "Thanks be to God, alleluia, alleluia."

Easter Sunday

The joy and enthusiasm that built up during the long and intense encounter of the Vigil cannot break off abruptly at its dismissal; it must spill over into further celebration. Moreover, in most of our parishes today— in the United States, at least—a large percentage of the parishioners are not present to participate in the vigil celebration. For them, the Easter Sunday becomes both the climax of the Sacred Triduum and the culmination of their lenten journey. After the homily both of these events are celebrated in the rite of Renewal of Baptismal Promises, which has been inserted into the *Sacramentary* (p. 209, "in the United States"). Thus at the present time Easter Sunday has a twofold character: It celebrates the baptismal character of Lent for some, and it is the overflow of sheer Easter joy for others.

Words adapted from Psalm 139 (erroneously listed as Psalm 138 in the *Sacramentary*) become a most appropriate Entrance Antiphon: "I have risen: I am with you once more; you placed your hand on me to keep me safe. How great is the depth of your wisdom, alleluia!" (*Sac.*, p. 208).[80] We are still rejoicing in our rebirth in Christ. Jesus of Nazareth is the one sent to accomplish God's merciful designs toward us. We are now more aware of the longing that the psalmist realized only dimly to be in the depth of his heart. The resurrection of Jesus makes him Christ, the Lord; that is, he has become the inner power motivating us. Hence the resurrection is not an historical event in the same manner as the passion and death are; rather, it is a state of being that makes Jesus to be Lord and that continues to expand and unfold in his Mystical Body until the end of time.

On this day we celebrate the transcendent and eschatological aspect of our life-in-Christ. We have already begun to live in the end-time. Because of our initiation into Christ there is something everlasting in everything we do when Christ is its motivation. It is no wonder, then, that we will need fifty days of celebration to allow the Paschal Mystery to penetrate our awareness and permeate all our responses. When we look at the implications of our initiation and renewal, we desire to channel its power into the deepest recesses of our hearts and into the hidden sources of our actions in order to develop a profound sensitivity to the Mystery of Christ in its twofold character: It has already been accomplished, and at the same time it remains to be carried out in our lives. Thus an "already-and-not-yet" mood pervades our celebration.

First Reading: Acts of the Apostles 10:34, 37-43

We begin with a reflection on the Word of God for this Sunday, and specifically with the First Reading from Acts. The event it records is as much a call to conversion for Peter as it is for Cornelius and his household. By entering the house of the centurion Cornelius, Peter finds himself called to act in a way that he, as a respectable Jew, would never have done on his own. Yet Peter's action is part of God's plan for universal salvation. As Peter enters into this plan, he adjusts the message of salvation to his listeners. Without reference to the Old Testament Scriptures, he preaches the *meaning* of the data of Jesus' life and conduct as well as of his death, resurrection, and post-resurrection appearances. Hence

Peter's words of salvation, given in the house of Cornelius, are also significant for us.

We, the community, identify with the proclamation. In fact, we realize that these words disclose the mystery we now *know* within. We have encountered Jesus Christ, the One anointed with the Holy Spirit and power. He has healed *us*; he has liberated *us* from the grip of the devil. Peter's witness is *real* for us today, and we know that the salvation proclaimed in this narrative has become an active force in our lives. Because "God raised him up on the third day," we too are empowered to be Christ's *chosen* witnesses. We become prophets. We have come to know God's forgiveness of our sins, and so we speak God's message and show that God's merciful designs have been accomplished within us; at the same time we are able to proclaim that message with added faith conviction.

We also learn adaptation firsthand in this pericope, and this is important. God calls us to proclaim the good news in any cultural circumstance in which we find ourselves. This requires us to be very sensitive both to the divine message and to the needs of the culture. Ignoring our culture's environment because the environment is sinful is not an attitude suitable for a disciple any more than is succumbing to a culture's allurements. We always need the judgment of the Good News upon us so that we will allow the risen Lord to call us forward.

Responsorial Psalm: Psalm 118:1-2, 16-17, 22-23

Since we have recognized and celebrated the power of Christ in our lives, we can sing of the greatness of the day that now transcends chronological time. It is the day beyond all limitations and confinements: "The right hand of the Lord has struck with power. . . . I shall not die, but live, and declare the works of the Lord." We share in the life and fate of the Lord. He was killed, hanged upon a tree; we were rejected stones by reason of our sins; but now our sins have not only been blotted out but have become *useful* to God in his act of re-creating us.

Admitting that we ourselves are stones once rejected but now used by the Lord allows compassion to arise within us: compassion for drug addicts, prostitutes, murderers, and any others whom we, in our sometimes shortsighted judgment, might deem to be unworthy of membership in our community. It is precisely through such persons that the mercy of God shines forth most vividly—both as God calls them to accept divine mercy and also as God calls the rest of us to drop our prejudices against them. Furthermore, we may also be holding some sinful weakness of our own under the "protective" covering of repression. If we uncover these dark areas in the presence of Jesus, he will heal us by his redeeming power. The pain we sustain in this struggle can become the "cornerstone" of our new knowledge of Jesus' presence with us and in us.

Second Reading: Colossians 3:1-4

The *Lectionary* offers a choice between two readings from Paul (Col. 3:1-4 and 1 Cor. 5:6-8). Both of them exhort us to become even more fully who we are. The selection from Colossians simply and directly exhorts us to set our hearts on the life Christ's victory achieved for us. When we allow the Mystery of Christ to penetrate more and more of our responses and attitudes, we will enjoy the fruits of that victory each day. The alternative reading from First Corinthians speaks of the difference that Christ makes in our motivation. The image of yeast is used to signify the old life of corruption and wickedness, while the unleavened bread refers to sincerity and truth.

Sequence

In the Sequence we sing of Christ's victory again in that piece of exquisite poetry known as the *Victimae Paschali*

Laudes. Christian experience, overflowing with joy and intensity, finds one of its deepest and most poetic expressions in this masterpiece. Striking contrasts such as "a Lamb the sheep redeems" and "the Prince of life, who died, reigns immortal" help to express and heighten our sentiments. Mary Magdalene witnesses to what she saw and also to the effect Jesus' revelation of himself as risen Lord had on her. Rare indeed is the translation or modern artistic musical setting that can express the depth of our religious experience as well as does this medieval Latin poem, particularly when enhanced by its Gregorian melody.

Gospel: John 20:1-9

The Alleluia, with its simple verse lauding Christ as our paschal sacrifice, leads us to the proclamation of the Gospel. This Gospel gives utterance to the love *(agape)* characteristic of Christians. Mary Magdalene cannot wait until daylight before she goes to anoint the body of her beloved. She becomes fearful and frantic when she notices that the grave is open. Peter and the other disciple show their eager love by running to the grave. The empty tomb is of itself certainly not a proof that Jesus has risen from the dead; only faith can reveal the resurrection. However, the empty tomb is a disconcerting reality that can move us to become more deeply aware. This is the path along which the author of today's Gospel leads us: from concern, to viewing the empty tomb, and finally to faith.

At first, it may seem odd that the reading makes so much of the shroud and the other cloths in which the body of Jesus had been wrapped.[81] However, when we view them in light of the initiation and renewal celebrated at the Vigil of Easter, we see their symbolic significance. In the ritual of baptism the shedding of old clothing symbolizes our break with the old Adam of sinfulness. After we have been buried with Christ in the waters of baptism, we receive new garments. The "death robes" in the tomb serve as a remembrance (anamnesis) of our call not to return to our old habits. The glorified Jesus has no further need of clothing. In the same way, we who have risen with him have no further need to cover ourselves with the protective clothing of our old insincerities.

The Gospel declares that the disciple whom Jesus loved "saw and believed." In other words, God was gradually bringing him to faith. Since many of us (the faithful) seem to have lived with dogma since our cradle days, we may not be accustomed to the notion of a gradual movement into faith. However, the Gospel's parenthetical "Remember, as yet they did not understand the Scripture that Jesus had to rise from the dead" clearly indicates that understanding of the event of initiation permeates our experiences very slowly. Although the sacramental celebration of baptism, confirmation, and Eucharist is indeed a *karios* (i.e., it transcends our chronology), still we need to be comforted and confronted, strengthened and energized many times before we will be moulded into an entirely new unity. It is also curious that the open tomb becomes an empty tomb within this Gospel, and that both images gradually become witnesses of the resurrection.

Easter Preface I

We have already mentioned a number of times that the Word, in its own way, makes memorial (anamnesis) of the Mystery it proclaims, and that the meaning of the event is even more fully disclosed and intensely celebrated in the Eucharistic Prayer. Thus in the Easter Preface I we find that our praise and thanks to the Father through Christ rests, first of all, on the realization that *now* is the time

. . . when Christ became our paschal sacrifice.
He is the true Lamb who took away the sins of the world.

By dying he destroyed our death;
by rising he restored our life. (*Sac.*, p. 415)

This narrative section of the Preface also colors the Eucharistic Prayer's central narrative. Christ continues his work of taking away the sins of the world in our own day. The newly baptized members in the assembly of the community become essential elements of our celebration. They reveal outwardly what is happening to all of us within. They are witnesses to the reality that Jesus the Lamb of God is still taking away the sins of the world and restoring us to life.

We have said that the liturgy of Easter Sunday brings the Sacred Triduum to a close; it also opens up the way for the period known as Easter Time. This is the period of the Mystagogia, and we see that, in a sense, the readings for the morning eucharistic celebration have already set us on this journey.

Thus the Sacred Triduum stands truly as the apex of the liturgical year. It has taken us the full circle of the Paschal Mystery. It began with the Eucharist of the Lord's Supper, then moved through the long period of waiting into the celebration of the Sacraments of Initiation. Now finally, amid great rejoicing, it opens the door to the journey through the Fifty Days.

Notes

1. *Calendarium Romanum*, Edito Typica (Typis Polyglottis Vaticanis, 1969), #18-19. Translation my own.
2. The Eastern Church has a strong "tradition" that the Parousia will indeed occur during the Easter Vigil.
3. The sciences of psychology and sociology could become "handmaids" of our faith union with God, somewhat in the same sense as philosophy served theology in the past. We need to be on guard, too, lest we confuse their identity with faith itself.
4. We cannot repeat too often that the attitude of praise and thanks is essential for any eucharistic celebration. See Chapter 4, pp. 147-149.

5. Council of Trent, Session XIII, *Decree on the Holy Eucharist,* c. 5.

6. For a consideration of the significance of the Eucharistic Prayer and of Eucharist as Christian meal, see the treatment of Eucharist as the climax of the process of initiation in Chapter 4, pp. 141-157.

7. Ambrose, *De Sacramentis,* Bk.3:4-5 quoted from E. C. Whitaker, *Documents of the Baptismal Liturgy* (London: S.P.C.K., 1960), p. 120.

8. See the historical development of the rite of reconciliation of penitents in Martimort, *L'Eglise,* op. cit., pp. 570-576. We have already called attention (p. 46, Chapter 2 note #2) to the excellent brief history of the development of the Order of Penitents in the Church during the fourth through sixth centuries. Note also: Nathan Mitchell, "Eucharistic Fellowship and Forgiveness," in *Rite of Penance: Commentaries,* vol. 3, op. cit., pp. 62-81; Louis Ligier, "The Origins of the Eucharistic Prayer: From the Last Supper to the Eucharist," in *Studia Liturgica* 9 (1973):161-185.

9. Forgiveness is truly a humiliating service rendered to another who has hurt us or done us an injustice. We must admit the hurt honestly and yet forgive for the sake of the other person. Even more, we have to assure forgiveness and reconciliation to our brothers and sisters for the sake of our relationship in the Body of Christ. We do this by the power Jesus gives us today: "As I have done, so you must do." (John 3:15). The example Jesus gives us in the Gospel is actualized in the close encounter of our total celebration. The Mystical Body is fed on this day in a unique manner, because the power to forgive is "contained" in the sacramental food and drink we receive.

10. The procession with the Holy Cross and the adoration has its origin in Jerusalem. Egeria, the Spanish nun who traveled so widely, gives us a vivid description of the Jerusalem liturgy. See: *Egeria: Diary of a Pilgrimage,* trans. G. E. Gingras (Ancient Christian Writers, 38; New York: Paulist Press, 1970). The *Trisagion* (translated: "Holy is God!" etc., *Sac.,* p. 163) is surely of Eastern origin. See Hermanus A. P. Schmidt, SJ, *Hebdomada Sancta* (Rome: Herder, 1957), p. 793.

11. A. Nocent, *The Liturgical Year,* vol. 3 (Collegeville, Minn.: Liturgical Press, 1977), p. 5.

12. See Moore, op. cit., pp. 13-16.
13. Anton Baumstark, *Comparative Liturgy* (London: A. R. Mowbray, 1958), pp. 35.
14. Moore, ibid., p. 16.
15. See Augustine: Sermon CXXXVI, I: Migne, *P. L.* 38, p. 745.
16. Moore, op. cit. passim, especially pp. 57-59.
17. Henri J. M. Nouwen, "The Monk and the Cripple," *America* (1980):208.
18. Nocent, op. cit., p. 93.
19. A. Hollardt, OP, "De spiritualiteit van stille saterdag," in *Tijdschrift voor Liturgie,* 64 (1980):74-83. I am greatly indebted to him for many insights included in this section.
20. Dennis Linn and Matthew Linn, *Healing for Life's Hurts: Healing Memories through the Five Stages of Forgiveness* (New York: Paulist Press, 1978). The entire book deals clearly and simply with the dark side of life and its value for the integrated person.
21. Cf. Jonah 2:1-11. The prayer of Jonah while he was in the belly of the whale indicates his faith in God and in God's victory. It points to the paradox that Jesus lived through.
22. A. Hollardt, op. cit. On p. 77 the author enumerates the images found in the apocryphal literature that refer to the descent of Jesus into the abode of the dead.
23. My translation of the following prayer for Vespers of Holy Saturday:

    Omnipotens sempiterne Deus,
    cujus unigenitus ad inferiora terrae descendit,
    unde et gloriosus ascendit,
    concede propitius,
    ut fideles tui, cum eo consepulti in baptismate,
    ipso resurgente, ad vitam proficiant sempiternam. Qui tecum.

    Liturgia Horarum juxta Ritum Romanum, v. 2, *Editio Typica* (Typis Polyglottis Vaticanis, 1972), p. 400.
24. *Liturgical Piety* (Notre Dame: University of Notre Dame Press, 1955), p. 188. Emphasis mine.
25. See Augustine, Sermon 272. Melissa Kay, ed., in the introduction to *It Is Your Own Mystery: A Guide to the Communion Rite* (Washington, D.C.: The Liturgical Conference, 1977), pp. 4-5, has an insightful expression of "Our Own Mystery."

26. See pp. 46-48 and 62-63.
27. We need always to bear in mind that the material becomes a symbol because it sets in motion the reality it reveals. And the Holy Spirit is the Proto-symbolizer who sets in motion the faith-reality.
28. We might consider other possibilities for lighting all the candles, depending on what a given assembly is concerned with. For example, there is something of value in having only the light of the Easter Candle during the Liturgy of the Word to get the "feel" that Christ as light of the world (John 8:12) illumines the entire Word of God which has gone before. Again, lighting the people's candles only at the Liturgy of Baptism—instead of blowing them out after the Easter Proclamation and then lighting them again—would give more unity and power to the single lighting of candles, both those of neophytes and those of the rest of the faithful, at the same time.
29. The adjective *necessarius* in late Latin often meant "inevitable" or "useful," rather than "indispensable." I would prefer to translate it "inevitable" or "beneficial."
30. See pp. 35, 45-46, 56.
31. See discussion of the incident at Meriba, pp. 55-56, and of that at Bethany, pp. 71-72.
32. For a good discussion of the choice of readings for this Vigil see: A. Chavasse, *Le Sacramentaire gélásien* (Turnai: Desclée et Cie, 1958), pp. 107-126; B. Botte, "Le choix des lectures de la vielle paschal," in *Questions liturgiques et paroissiales* 33 (1952):65-70.
33. Robert Taft, SJ, "The Liturgical Year," *Worship* 55 (1981):12.
34. See Baars, op. cit., passim.
35. For a detailed description of "type" and "antitype," see Jean Danielou, SJ, *The Bible and the Liturgy* (Notre Dame: University of Notre Dame Press, 1956), pp. 4-9.
36. See Peter Fink, SJ, "Three Languages of Worship," in *Worship* 52:567.
37. This prayer is found in all the ancient manuscripts: See Placide Bruylants, OSB, *Les Oraisons du Missel Romain*, I-II, *Etudes Liturgique* I (Louvain: Centre de Documentation et d'Information Liturgiques, 1952), I, p. 41; II, p. 66, #211. Note: Something of the concrete imagery of the Latin text has been lost in our present English translation. The omission of the phrase "the right hand of God" constitutes a substantial loss in itself.

38. Lucien Deiss, SSSp, *God's Word and God's People* (College-ville, Minn.: Liturgical Press, 1976), p. xxiii.
39. We need to keep in mind that the term *sacrament* stands for the celebration of our ongoing initiation *into* the passage of Jesus from death to new life.
40. See Ira Progoff, *The Well and the Cathedral,* new enlarged edition (New York: Dialogue House Library, 1977), p. 107 and passim. Progoff provides a process by which we are enabled to reach the depths of our persons, and there come to realize how we are united with other persons. Such awareness can be a firm support to our faith-awareness in the body of Christ.
41. See P. Bruylants, OSB, op. cit., p. 71, #232. This research shows how the prayer in question was found in a number of sources and was used after different readings. It was used for the Easter Vigil and for the Pentecost Vigil as well. Unfortunately, much of the prayer's visual and tactile imagery has been lost in the present ICEL translation.
42. See A. Blaise, *Dictionnaire Latin-Français des Auteurs Chrétiens* (Paris: Librairie des Méridiens, 1954), p. 823. He cites Gaudentius as calling Christ the *tranquillator,* "the one who quells the storm."
43. See prayers after Second and Third Readings, both of which refer to increasing the number of true sons of Abraham through baptism.
44. Frank L. Cross, ed., *St. Cyril of Jerusalem's Lectures on the Christian Sacraments* (London: S.P.C.K., 1960), pp. 12-39 and pp. 53-80. When St. Cyril speaks to the newly baptized, he refers to their triple submergence in the water as an experience of the death and darkness of the tomb; and he refers to their emergence from the dark waters as their resurrection with Christ.
45. Ibid., p. 54.
46. An interesting aside for us in the 1980s would be to take note of how all three Synoptic Gospels portray the first appearance of the risen Christ to women. While we struggle with the debate over equal rights for women, we might do well to ask Christ to heal this wound in our human lives, and to be on guard against the competitiveness and chauvinism that might develop within the proponents of either side of this question.

47. Pierre Jounel, "The Bible in the Liturgy," in *The Liturgy and the Word of God* (Collegeville, Minn.: Liturgical Press, 1959), p. 19. Emphasis mine.

48. See 1 John 5:6-8 for John's view of this.

49. Louis Bouyer, *The Paschal Mystery* (Chicago: Henry Regenery Co., 1950), p. 303.

50. Quoted from Alexander Schmemann, *Of Water and the Spirit* (Crestwood, N.Y.: St. Vladimir's Seminary Press, 1974), p. 49.

51. See pp. 121-122.

52. Raimundo Panikkar, Preface to *Teresa of Avila, the Interior Castle* (New York: Paulist Press, 1979), p. xii.

53. In liturgy, as in life in general, the gesture of laying on hands may be unclear. It is either a sign of protection or warding off evil, or it is a symbol of affirmation and enhancement. The gesture used in confirmation belongs to the latter category.

54. For a perceptive insight into the source of our confusion about the sacrament of confirmation today, see Nathan Mitchell, OSB, "Dissolution of the Rite of Christian Initiation," in *Made, Not Born: New Perspectives on Christian Initiation and the Catechumenate*, Murphy Center for Liturgical Research (Notre Dame: University of Notre Dame Press, 1975), pp. 50-82, especially pp. 74-75.

55. See Philippe Rouillard, "From Human Meal to Christian Eucharist," *Worship* 52 (September 1978):425-439, and 53 (January 1979):40-56. This article is a translation from the French original that appeared in *Notitiae*, nos. 131-132 (1977). This excellent article gives a detailed account of the religious significance of meals in the Old and New Testaments together with a bit of the historical development.

56. See pp. 92-93.

57. Louis Bouyer, *Eucharist*, p. 30.

58. The sample *berakah* below contains the four structural elements of which we have been speaking. The following prayer is taken from the *Didache*, an early Christian document dating from the end of the first century. (We cannot at this point enter into the controversy over the precise nature of this document.) The text quoted here is taken from Gregory Dix, *The Shape of the Liturgy* (London: Dacre Press, 1964), p. 90. We allowed the text to stand as it appears in his work.

We give thanks unto Thee, our Father, for the life and knowledge, which Thou didst make known unto us through Jesus Thy servant; to Thee be glory forever. As this broken bread was scattered upon the tops of the mountains and being gathered became one, so gather Thy church from the ends of the earth into Thy kingdom; for Thine is the glory and the power through Jesus Christ forever.

In this sample the various parts—laudatory address, mentioning a wonderful deed of God, petition and doxology—are easily discernible. The word "doxology" means "a formulation of praise to God": thus the "Glory to the Father . . . ," the "Glory to God in the highest," the phrase "to thee be glory forever," and the final sentence of the prayer quoted above are all doxologies. You may recognize the prayer quoted from the *Didache* from the well-known song "Father, We Thank Thee" (Genevan Psalter, 1543, translated by F. Bland Tucker, Copyright 1964, World Library of Sacred Music, Cincinnati, Ohio); it appears in a number of song books.

59. Section 55. From now on all references to this document which appears in the *Sacramentary* pp. 17*-47*, will be indicated by GI and the section number.

60. Mark Searle, "The Christian Community: Evangelized and Evangelizing," in *Emmanuel* 86 (December 1980):610.

61. Louis Bouyer, *Liturgical Piety* (Notre Dame, Ind.: University of Notre Dame Press, 1955), p. 119.

62. See Edward Kilmartin, SJ, "A Modern Approach to the Word," op. cit., p. 74. Juan Llopis, "The Liturgy Celebrates God's Presence in the World and His Invitation to Man," in Herman Schmidt, SJ, ed., *Liturgy in Transition*, Concilium 62 (New York: Herder and Herder, 1971), p. 124; David Tracey, "The Public Character of Systematic Theology," in *Theology Digest*, 26 (1979):404ff.

63. In addition to the statement in the *Constitution on the Liturgy, Gaudium et Spes* tells us that we need to bear in mind the consequences of the fact that the world has passed from a static to a more dynamic concept of reality (#5). We have not even begun to recognize the implications that this change has for our awareness of symbols in the liturgy.

64. Bernard Bro, OP, *The Spirituality of the Sacraments: Doctrine and Practice for Today* (New York: Sheed and Ward, 1968), p. 43.

65. Robert Ledogar, *Acknowledgement: Praise Verbs in Early Greek Anaphoras* (Rome: Herder, 1968), p. 167. Ledogar comes to the conclusion that the meaning of all the praise verbs could be gathered under the one concept of *acknowledgment*.

66. Alexander Shmemann, *For the Life of the World: Sacraments & Orthodoxy* (Crestwood, N.Y.: St. Vladimir's Seminary Press, 1973), p. 39.

67. The Latin word for *restore* in this Preface is *reparare*, which means "to restore through salvation." Thus it means more than simply bringing the natural human life back sinless. It includes the concept of a "new" creation.

68. GI #55; Faith and Order Paper #73 of the World Council of Churches, Geneva, Switzerland, 1975, calls this element "the words of Christ's institution of the sacrament according to the New Testament tradition" in *One Baptism, One Eucharist and Mutually Recognized Ministry*, p. 26.

69. We have barely scratched the surface of the meaning of the word *benedixit*, "he said the blessing." The word includes praise to God; it means acknowledging the wonderful deeds of God in such a way that those deeds become present.

70. See Robert Taft, SJ, "The Liturgical Year" in *Worship* 55 (January 1981):1.

71. There is ample evidence that the Last Supper was a Passover meal; it surely had evident paschal overtones. See especially Jeremias, *The Eucharistic Words of Jesus* (Philadelphia: Fortress Press, 1977). For evidence to the contrary see A. Jaubert, *The Date of the Last Supper* (New York: Alba House, 1965).

72. See Ellebracht, op. cit., p. 188 and passim to discover how the language of Prayers over the Gifts and Postcommunions indicates that the entire liturgical celebration, and not simply the reception of Holy Communion, effect the divine gifting.

73. Peter Fink, SJ, "Three Languages of Worship," in *Worship* 52:569. See also the Easter Proclamation: "Night truly blessed when heaven is wedded to earth. . . ."

74. Cornelius A. Bouman, in his unpublished notes (Nijmegen: Catholic University of Holland), clarified the faith content of the epiclesis in its earliest form, as a recognition of the Holy Spirit's action on the eucharistic meal in both

its aspects, i.e., as food and as social bonding. See also Gregory Dix, *The Shape of the Liturgy* (London: Dacre Press, 1964), pp. 277-290, particularly pp. 289-290, where he indicates how the invocation of the Holy Spirit is in line with Paul's word about "showing forth" the death of the Lord (see 1 Cor 11:26); Cyprian Vaggaggini, *Theological Dimensions of the Liturgy* (Collegeville, Minn.: Liturgical Press, 1976), p. 226n states that the mention of the Holy Spirit was not formalized into a consecratory epiclesis till the end of the third century.

75. Schmemann, op. cit., pp. 44-45.
76. This position is held by J. A. Jungmann. See *The Place of Christ in Liturgical Prayer*, 2nd rev. ed. (New York: Alba House, 1964), pp. 202-205. This source includes some explanation of the controversy which Jungmann's position has aroused.
77. Fink, op. cit., p. 571.
78. See Rouillard, op. cit., p. 435.
79. George Malone, SJ, *Inscape* (Dennville, N.Y.: 1978), p. 133.
80. This Entrance Song is an example of how words from Scripture sometimes came to be adapted to liturgical usage. Verses 17 and 18 of Psalm 139 read: "How weighty are your designs, O God; how vast the sum of them! Were I to recount them, they would outnumber the sands, did I reach the end of them I should be still with you" (NAB). The Latin *exsurexi*—"reach the end"—has become *resurrexi*—"I arose." And the rest was adjusted to fit. Note: There is an alternative entrance verse in the present *Sacramentary*.
81. In a perceptive article in *Vocabulaire de Théologie Biblique* (Paris: Les Editions du Cerf, 1962) pp. 1098-1103, Edgar Houlotte, SJ, notes the variety of meanings which clothing has in the Bible. This passage summarizes the four-and-one-half-page article: "Le vêtement est désormais le signe d'une dualité: Il affirme la dignité de l'homme déchu et la possibilité de revêtir une gloire perdue." "Clothing is a sign of a certain duality: It affirms the dignity of fallen man and the possibility of his being clothed again in the glory he lost" (p. 1101; translation mine).

5

A REFLECTION ON THE EVENT OF THE PASCHAL MYSTERY

Easter Time:
The Mystagogia—Ongoing Initiation into Christ

Any significant event needs time to be absorbed. We require time for reflection if we wish to integrate what has happened and allow it to influence our lives. This is certainly true of the event celebrated during Triduum. The threefold rite of initiation—baptism, confirmation, and Eucharist—constitutes an event of the first magnitude in our lives. We anticipated it by a long preparation and experienced its unfolding with intense, impassioned joy. Now is the time to absorb all that has taken place in our "Christ-ening." We need more than a week and a day (an octave) for this maturation. And so, to assimilate the Easter passage into our daily living, we celebrate Easter with an "octave" that lasts for a "week of weeks" plus one day. We need these fifty days *each year*—particularly the eight Sunday celebrations—to allow ourselves, along with the newly baptized, to move forward with the special insights and graces that this year's celebration has provided. Hence these Sundays are truly Sundays *of*, not *after*, Easter, and the Roman Calendar of 1969 names them thus (#23).[1]

We have stressed initially (in Chapter 1) that organisms build their structures, their life-support systems, from within. Throughout the ensuing pages we have been using terms like *journey* and *breakthrough* as analogues to name the process, the life course, through which God has lovingly been calling us during Lent and Triduum. Breakthroughs have occurred along our journey toward *faith* and toward our Easter passage with Christ into *new* life. This new life is not static. Hence it needs time to be assimilated, to be lived. We need to affirm it again and again, and we need to reflect long and lovingly on what has occurred in order to allow it to penetrate all our faculties.

The structure to which we look to support the inner reflective life of Easter Time is the *Rite of Christian Initiation of Adults* (RCIA). The Introduction to the RCIA states that during Easter Time " . . . the community and the neophytes move forward together, meditating on the Gospel, sharing in the eucharist, and performing works of charity. In this way *they understand* the paschal mystery more fully and *bring it into their lives more and more*" (#37; emphasis mine). The section of the rite under consideration here is known as the Period of Postbaptismal Cathechesis or Mystagogia.² We need to dwell further on the concept of Postbaptismal Catechesis, which in this book we will call "Postinitiatory Catechesis," because confirmation and Eucharist also belong to the initiatory journey.

A profound rationale underlies the ancient practice of giving what looks like an "instruction on the rites" *after* the neophytes' initiation. Some may interpret this "post" instruction as evidence that in the third and fourth centuries candidates received the sacraments without knowing what they were doing, but this is not the case. Nor is it true to say that the so-called *disciplina arcani* (the Early Christian practice of barring the uninitiated from the Church's ritual celebrations) was the primary motive for delaying explanations. Bishops such as Cyril of Jerusalem and Ambrose of Milan were not acting out of fear that some intruder might misinterpret the sacred actions. Their interest was primarily at the other end of the process: They were concerned that those who wished to be initiated should be authentically committed to Christ;

then they would not experience rituals as empty motions.

The early Church realized that after the elect came to know the death and rising of Jesus in their own persons, they would want to celebrate this gift in suitable gestures. Such spontaneous movement to express and celebrate in gestures and other symbols takes place in the development of any interpersonal relationship. We have an example of this on the faith level in the story related in Acts 8:26-39, where, after Philip opened the Scriptures about the Suffering Servant, the Ethiopian official of Queen Candace requested baptism. Although it stands to reason that certain basic gestures symbolize identical movements to nearly all people, still today we tend to explain them and encourage candidates for baptism, or for any other sacrament, to "live themselves *into* the ritual." Not so with Ambrose or Chrysostom and others. Their *Mystagogical Catechesis* were reflections on what had taken place; they were expressions of loving admiration *after the fact.*[3]

The Period of Postinitiatory (Postbaptismal) Catechesis or Mystagogia today seems to have a significantly different character from what it had in the fourth century. When Ambrose and Cyril undertook to lead the newly initiated through reflection and continuing celebration, they confined their observations to the "concentrated" form of the Word as it appeared in the ritual gestures. Our walk with the newly initiated seems to be freer. We emphasize the scripture texts in their entirety as anamneses of the Easter passage. The Church has arranged the scripture readings, particularly those of Cycle A, in such a way that they lead us through the process of learning to recognize—coming to know—the risen Lord in our day-to-day living. In its introduction to the Period of the Postbaptismal Catechesis the RCIA stresses broad realities such as the "new frequenting of the sacraments [which] enlightens the neophytes' understanding of the holy scriptures and also increases their knowledge of men and develops the experience in the community itself." It even recognizes the mission of the neophytes to renew the vision of the faithful and give them a new impetus (RCIA #39).

Before reflecting on each of the Sundays of Easter, we will outline the perspective from which we will make our observations. In the first place, the communion that has been realized within the assembly by the paschal event (Easter passage) makes this gathering a newly constituted community. This is true by reason of the initiation of new members into it, and it is also true because other members have renewed themselves and have made new commitments to conversion.

Secondly, this newly constituted community becomes a living symbol of the entire span of life within the Church. Life-in-Christ is a never-ending process, and it proceeds through characteristic stages of growth. These stages are not hard-and-fast compartments. Rather, each one intertwines in a living way with the following one, while maintaining something of the preceding one. Thus there is continuity within the community even as it attains new levels of growth. Finally, since shifts and apparent overlappings also seem to take place, they give the impression that reversals sometimes happen in the process. We will see this more clearly as we reflect on the scripture passages of the various Sundays of Easter Time. Finally, we will be concentrating more on the inner life and growth of faith than on the structures of the specific liturgies. This concentration will hold true in our discussion of the feasts of Ascension and Pentecost as well.

Second Sunday of Easter

On this Sunday we are still very close to the peak celebration of Triduum. As we look at today's three scripture readings, we detect several ways for Christians to recognize the risen Lord and to enter into relationship with him. Today's readings reveal that through our own woundedness (John 20:19-31), through the shared living faith-life within our community (Acts 2:42-47), and finally, through patient endurance of trials and persecution for the sake of the Gospel (1 Peter 1:3-9), the efficacious power of Christ dwelling within weak human beings is the constant marvel of Christian life. It is no wonder that joy so consistently breaks through it.

Gospel: John 20:19-31

Important aspects of Christian life are woven into this artistically constructed gospel story. The author of the Gospel sets the action of the narrative on the first day of the week—the day on which Christians gathered, and continue to gather, to celebrate and meet the risen Lord. Fear—symbolized so well in the locked doors—does not deter the Lord's entry into the assembly. The same remains true for us, even when fear fills our hearts and locks us behind doors of non-communication or other masks. When Jesus makes himself present, he banishes fear and replaces it with his own peace. Sometimes, when we face political injustice, oppression, or large-scale, unjust economic practices, fear may be widespread. Even in the face of such fear, however, Jesus still shows his presence. If hope and courage and martyrdom emerge when we would expect only despair, then we *know* the Lord is present. For the peace born of such hope is from the risen Lord.[4]

The reading goes on to focus the history of human existence in the expression "he breathed on them." On the First Sunday of Lent in the second creation story from Genesis, we heard how Adam became a living being when God breathed life into his nostrils. After the resurrection, in a new creative act, the new Adam breathes the new life of the Holy Spirit into the disciples and into us. In so doing, Jesus reveals both the core of the Gospel's message and the heart of the Church's mission. And since that message is one of forgiveness and that mission is one of reconciliation, the peace Jesus grants puts an end to our alienation from God.

Two instances of irony enhance this story and give it more power to affect us. The first instance centers around the glorified wounds of Jesus. Since Jesus is now glorified, why consider his wounds at all? They are the mark of his condemnation and death. However, after Christ's passage they become the marks by which the disciples recognize the Lord, but not merely in a physical or material sort of way. Rather, the glorified wounds serve as signs to bring the disciples face to face with the mystery of the saving power Christ's passage generated within them. The various signs we use in the liturgy today perform that same role for us.

The second instance of irony focuses on Thomas and grants us an even deeper recognition of Jesus as Lord. Since we are familiar with the story, we enjoy looking at Thomas' bumbling. At the same time however, the Gospel also puts *us* through Thomas' paces of moving from brash incredulity to full faith. Thomas' story becomes ours. When he places his finger into the nail marks and his hand into Jesus' side, Thomas' unbelief changes into faith, and his hard heart becomes flesh. Thomas experiences a *radical* change. When such a change happens in us or among us, we know that a conversion has taken place, a conversion that brings us into contact with the reality—the new life—Christ's Easter passage has accomplished. The proclamation of this Gospel—along with the presence of the newly converted neophytes— helps us realize how God's Word creates new life in the assembly.

First Reading: Acts of the Apostles 2:42-47

The First Reading describes the primitive Christian community as it was brought together by the apostles' instruction. Although its members continued to go to the temple area together to pray, they also broke bread— celebrated Eucharist—in their homes. The reading clearly emphasizes the simplicity of the early Christians' lives, not the structure of their community. People around them who noticed the joy breaking forth from their inner peace sought to join them—the Holy Spirit binding them together. The fact that they held "all things in common" evidences that the Holy Spirit was their bonding power.

Today, through scientific studies in sociology and psychology, we are becoming more aware of the influence we have on one another in community. We realize how we are able to choose the way we want to act when we have strong community support. Above all, as Christians we are beginning to recognize that this power among us is a significant symbol of the activity and power of the Holy Spirit, who binds us into one. The very existence of such community, then, witnesses to the presence and activity of the risen Savior.

Responsorial Psalm: Psalm 118:2-4, 13-15, 22-24

Our response begins, "Give thanks to the Lord for he is good, his love is everlasting." The verses selected from Psalm 118 stress God's conquest of sin. They portray the struggle, the being near to falling, and then the victory. Our wonderment over the rock rejected by the builders becoming the cap-stone parallels our admiration at the presence of Christ's glorified wounds.

Second Reading: 1 Peter 1:3-9

The first half of the Second Reading is a paean of praise for our new life in Christ.[5] Terms such as *new birth, resurrection,* and *imperishable inheritance* evidence the way Peter's audience viewed the life into which they were initiated. Indeed, "there is cause for rejoicing here!"

The second half of this selection recognizes that the mystery of redemption takes time to penetrate our attitudes and habits of behavior. Although these behaviors do not become the center of attention, neither are they blithely ignored or repressed. On the contrary, Peter admits that Christians suffer the "distress of many trials." Nevertheless, these trials serve to enhance and give luster to the new life of faith. The reading moves from considering trials to affirming the loving God, and then goes on to the theme of the day: "Blest are they who have not seen and have believed" (see John 20:30 and 1 Pet. 1:8). Indeed, God blesses us and touches us with glory even in this mortal life "because [we] are achieving faith's goal, [our] salvation." Already blessed, touched, and redeemed by God, we struggle to make redemption fully effective in our lives. Such is the eschatological character of the Christian life.

Third Sunday of Easter

The Sundays of Easter celebrate the Church's deeper living out of the Paschal Mystery. Each week they reveal another facet of the Christian life, and they break open its meaning in our liturgical celebration. Today's celebration provides yet another remarkable way for us to enter into Christ's Easter passage. Its Liturgy of the Word not only witnesses our movement into the Paschal Mystery but also sheds light on how we come to recognize the risen Lord "in the breaking of the bread."

Gospel: Luke 24:13-35

We begin once more with the Gospel. Many a Christian—if indeed not every one—has agonized over the realization that the presence of the risen Lord is by no means always evident in our attitudes and behavior. We encounter many situations in which we fail to see him at all. However, the risen Lord is not someone we can ignore, especially after we have initially experienced his presence or after he has awakened hopes within us. Today's "good news" addresses itself to this anxiety residing in the hearts of many disciples.

Frequently the Christian community finds itself moving from hope to discouragement in close succession, especially during periods of trial and suffering. Such experiences enable us to experience better the story of the two disciples on their way to Emmaus. Like them, we look to Jesus for liberation from oppressive systems; with them, we also view Jesus as a prophet powerful in word and deed. Our expectations, however, like theirs, very often do not go far enough. Liberation from slavery—be it economic, political, or even psychological—is not enough to satisfy our longings if we consider liberation only in the sense of being removed from some oppression. The "third day," the day of hope and newness, may bring us a vision of angels, but very often it does not reveal the risen Lord. There is only one way to find him, and that is by going *through* and *beyond* death with him and in him.

The story, as told by Luke, makes Jesus' words effective as he brings the Suffering Servant theology to bear upon the situation of the two disciples. Although the disciples' situation of having Jesus walking with them and their not recognizing him seems ironic, we also often fail to recognize the Lord's presence, and Jesus' words strike home: "Did not the Messiah *have* to undergo all this so as to enter into his glory?" (Emphasis mine.) It may be easier for us to reflect on how much we resemble Cleopas and his companion than it is to hear firsthand the rebuke: "What little sense you have! How slow you are to believe . . . !" and yet Jesus speaks these same words to us today. Like the disciples' hearts, our hearts are also burning, and we are eager to enter into "the breaking of the bread" with the Lord, for we know that being able to recognize the risen Lord must come to us as a gift. *We cannot make it happen.* (We will return to this passage after we have considered the other two readings, lest we lose the continuity of the mystery as today's liturgy proclaims it.)

First Reading: Acts of the Apostles 2:14, 22-28

In this First Reading we find some of the same facets of the mystery of Jesus as we found in the Gospel. Peter begins by calling attention to the miracles, signs, and wonders that Jesus performed. Peter is speaking to his fellow Israelites, and he is eager to show that God controls and directs the entire life and death of Christ in order to fulfill his own plans. It is important to note that Peter says: "God . . . raised him up again." These words declare that we too can expect God to raise us up to new life in his Son. Peter then quotes Psalm 16 to demonstrate how the Scriptures have been fulfilled in Christ. The essential message of the passage quoted is that the power that saves Jesus from death is his personal relationship with his Father. Death—even the death that is sin—is not final. This is true simply and solely because God will personally *not allow* his "faithful one" to see corruption.

Responsorial Psalm: Psalm 16:1-2, 5, 7-8, 9-10, 11

Psalm 16, our response to the First Reading, reveals how profoundly the assembly is involved in the message of proclamation. Resurrection actually contains the glorification of all humanity in the person of the God-man, since he is intimately related to the ever-living God.

Second Reading: 1 Peter 1:17-21

In the Second Reading we hear another selection from this early Christian baptismal catechesis in which we are reminded that we have been delivered from our "futile way of life," not by any monetary gift but by the blood of Christ who was chosen before the world began. The reading exhorts us to live according to the new life we have received. Since this life is vastly different from that of the culture around us, we can compare ourselves to sojourners in a strange land. We have been redeemed from the futile way of life around us by the greatest price anyone could possibly pay: the supreme act of love of Jesus the spotless lamb. Even more, we share now in the transcendent life of Jesus, who has been glorified by his Father. Therefore our life-in-Christ is essentially "other," different from human life without Christ. The Holy Spirit engenders a new motivation within us; and sin, which proceeds from unredeemed humanness, no longer has a stranglehold on us.

At this point we can consider more deeply the inner movement going on between the Liturgy of the Word and the Liturgy of the Eucharist that makes it one event. The gospel reading follows an inner process that no doubt is the vitality that very early shaped the Christian celebration of the Lord's Day. It narrates the flow of what was happening within the hearts of Cleopas and his companion. For us, and for any who meet Christ today, this text reveals that this same process is also a *present reality*, a divine-human reality that comes into being as we allow ourselves to be present to God and to what God is accomplishing within our assembly. The inner motive force within the Word effects what the Word says. The Word reveals or discloses a wonderful deed: what God is accomplishing in us when we listen. This is what makes it a memorial or anamnesis. We have noted the relationship between Word and Sacrament several times as we studied the Prefaces in relation to the Gospels of the various Sundays of Lent. Today's gospel text illustrates how Word becomes Sacrament for us today.

Through contemplative openness—by our being aware of the movements within ourselves and by being able to recognize what God is saying to us—we come to *know* the divine-human happening as it occurs today in our communal worship. As we become involved in the story, we notice that it moves us—*lures us* might be a more accurate phrase—to commit ourselves to the Lord. When we feel inclined to say to the two disciples, "Open your eyes! Christ is with you right now!" our own hearts begin to burn, and we are inwardly readied, whether consciously or not, to invite Jesus to abide with us. This does not happen until we have let ourselves become vulnerable to the story's "punch line": "Did not the Messiah *have* to undergo all this so as to enter into his glory?" (Emphasis mine.)

Storytelling as an art form is eminently suited to be the vehicle to carry God's message to us and to bring us into God's message. As an art form, the story utilizes Jesus' interpretation of "every passage of Scripture which referred to him" to fill up the time required to travel the miles between Jerusalem and Emmaus. As a faith proclamation, the interpretation indicates the continuity of God's saving plan; and during our celebration today it also allows Jesus to put us through the process of absorbing the truth that he explodes in our bewildered hearts when he says that the Messiah *had to undergo all this*. When discouragement restrains us from recognizing Jesus, and we say with the disciples, "We were hoping that he was the one," we are unable to adopt a different attitude all at once.

On the other hand, even though in the midst of pain we say with the disciples, " . . . but him [Jesus]…[we] did not see," the hope of resurrection keeps tugging at our hearts. The Holy Spirit sharpens this conflict and motivates us to ask Jesus to abide with us. The nagging self-hatred brought on by discouragement suddenly shows up as part of a mighty deed of God. What was an obstacle hindering the two disciples from accepting God's saving plan, because that plan included the death of Jesus, now helps them to recognize Jesus. The same is true for us. The risen Lord does not give his disciples—or us, the worshipping community—a *reason* not to be discouraged. Rather, he transforms unbelief and fear-induced helplessness into love and enthusiasm. Such is Jesus' wonderful deed for this Sunday, a deed we understand fully only when we share the Table of the Lord.

When he had seated himself with them to eat, he took bread, pronounced the blessing, then broke the bread and began to distribute it to them. With that their eyes were opened and they recognized him . . . in the breaking of the bread.

By its very nature, the meal setting of the Eucharist calls us to be committed to one another. It calls for an *abiding* presence, a being comfortable with one another. This kind of presence becomes uniquely integrating for human beings. Also, even though we may seem to be the ones who are inviting the Lord, it becomes immediately clear that Jesus of Nazareth—once dead, now risen— is the host and that we are *his* guests. The Word has personally led us through the process of coming to realize that the Messiah *had* to suffer in order to enter into his glory. At the meal we experience that we are in the presence of the *glorified* Lord and are being nourished at his own table.

Jesus' supreme act of self-giving is no longer bounded by the time nor the space nor the other circumstances in which he first offered his body and blood for us. Today we encounter his saving act of love in our ritual memorial. At the eucharistic table we share the food and drink that have become the real presence of him who inflames our hearts. To say that we *know* him, or as we have shown elsewhere, that we *acknowledge*[6] him in "the breaking of the bread" is to admit that his presence is by no means a static one. Jesus is personally interacting with us and calling forth a response from us.

Our ritual celebration, then, is replete with the movement that God directed in order to invite human beings into intimate union with himself. We need to reflect deeply and together on this day's Gospel in order to experience how closely we identify with what it reveals. Such reflection will help us always to be on our guard not to settle in and allow our celebration to become an ossified ritual. It may be helpful to summarize the process once again. Our encounter with God in Christ is intensely personal. It happens, first of all, and is shaped initially, when the Word is proclaimed in the assembly. It is a meeting that takes place in dialogue. The encounter continues to grow, and it takes a definitive shape in the ritual action of eating and drinking. The Eucharistic Prayer, which is actually a concentrated form of the Word, reveals the meal as the fullest expression of our meeting with God.

When we share this encounter with full awareness and commitment, we can reflect again how our hearts are burning within us, and then, with enthusiasm born of that experience, we can tell others what has happened to us—what the experience of a wonderful deed of God is like—and thus begin to evangelize them.

Fourth Sunday of Easter

First Reading: Acts of the Apostles 2:14, 36-41

Our life-in-Christ consists in our becoming always more aware of new areas of growth in intimacy and commitment. After reflecting on the mystery proclaimed in last Sunday's celebration—particularly as it was revealed in the scripture readings—and allowing it to permeate our consciousness, we must experience delight and a sense of "rightness" when we hear Peter's first words in today's reading: "Let the whole house of Israel know beyond any doubt that God has made both Lord and Messiah this Jesus whom you crucified." What could be more congruent with the identity of the Church renewed in the Paschal Sacraments than this exhortation? Such is God's economy: God allows divine forgiveness to work itself out right in the heart of human meanness. This is what gives the proclamation of the Word its inner power to move us, for when we come face to face with the Crucified, we realize that we are crucifying ourselves when we sin. This pericope delineates how we see the reality of our sin. It proclaims the change of heart involved, and it opens the way for the entire community to enter even more fully into the reading itself.

Jesus actually becomes Messiah for us today when, deeply shaken, we ask with Peter's listeners, "What are we to do, brothers?" God brings us into the inner movement of forgiveness that makes possible the complete reversal of our lives. The words that command us to reform and be baptized are words of power; they fill us with the power that enables us to fulfill them.

Peter's response to the above query, "Save yourselves from this generation which has gone astray," is uniquely apropos for us today. The One who has been crucified is the One who dissipates sin when he forgives it. We approach baptism, then, "in the name of Jesus Christ, that [our] sins may be forgiven." Every era of history has its own way of tempting us to become culture-bound, as if such binding could bring salvation. The way of culture—be it having enough money in the bank, returning evil for evil, setting up endless agencies, maintaining first-strike military power, looking to the next technological advance for final answers, or whatever— seems so practical, so logical, and even necessary. We need liberation from our culture in order to be able to discern where its assumptions fail. Therefore, although we need liberation so that we may be among the those "added" on this day, we also need to be liberated from our culture so that we may be able to incarnate the Gospel in it.

Responsorial Psalm: Psalm 23:1-3, 3-4, 5, 6

The Responsorial Psalm gives us the time and the words to savor the new hope that is coming alive within us. We reiterate over and over that with the Lord for our shepherd we will lack nothing. We have sufficient food, drink, security from danger, and companionship at table. There is a sense of permanence of relationship with the Lord too: "I shall dwell in the house of the Lord for years to come." As we have mentioned several times, the function

of the Responsorial Psalm is to affirm the messages proclaimed in the First Reading and to function as the assembly's response to the entire Liturgy of the Word.
Psalm 23 appears in this capacity in the liturgy quite
often. The message of the First Reading and of the
Gospel colors its use today. The confidence that this
psalm engenders takes on a specific character of hope
today: hope that the power of our celebration will elicit
essential conversion to Christ. By essential conversion
we do not mean the change of heart that is preliminary
to baptism. Rather, the term is used to indicate that
Christian conversion at any stage in life is always gift,
always surpasses moral perfection and psychological
growth, and flows from the new life we possess.

Gospel: John 10:1-10

The Responsorial Psalm leads us into a consideration of
today's Gospel; for, like the psalm, the Gospel proclaims
the radical nature or the transcendence of our commitment to Christ. Jesus calls himself the gate to the sheepfold. To enter through him means to discover that on
the other side of the gate, i.e., in the sheepfold, everything in our life is reversed, and that we are moving into
fuller life. When we realize that the Good Shepherd
knows us and that we know him (gospel verse, John 10:14),
we begin to live an entirely new kind of life. We do more
than talk about our encounter with the risen Lord. In
our celebration we make anamnesis or memorial of what
we have come to *know* experientially. We make present
the reality of the meaning of our life which Christ has
revealed to us. Thus, our memorial helps us commit
ourselves to the risen Lord.

The divine life of which we partake can be mediated
to us only by Christ. Only Christ can be so close to us
that we recognize his voice within our very hearts. When
he enters to lead his faithful to green pastures, he "walks
in front of them, and the sheep follow him." These words
evoke within our hearts both the spirit of the Suffering

Servant who was led by God, and Jesus' own words as well: "If a man wishes to come after me, he must . . . take up his cross, and follow in my steps." (Mark 8:34 NAB) The only way we will be able to recognize his voice is by following him. To be called by name implies intimacy; and the closer our intimacy with our Shepherd, the fuller will be the life we enjoy. Jesus' words "I came that they might have life and have it to the full" reveal the meaning of Jesus as the gate. Symbol becomes person. Jesus Christ is our access to power as well as our leader.

Second Reading: 1 Peter 2:20-25

" . . . but now you have returned to the shepherd, the guardian of your souls." On some Sundays the relationships among the three readings seems so evident we must be cautious lest the connections we make be too superficial. Today's Second Reading seems to imply that we must follow the Good Shepherd to our own Calvaries. Peter tells us that Christ has "left [us] an example, to have [us] follow in his footsteps." Peter, however, is not encouraging external imitation or mimicking when he speaks of "example." Rather, he is proclaiming that God is not only empowering us to discover ourselves as created in the divine image, and not only reinstating us to the condition we had before the fall, but actually is giving us a share in Jesus' own sonship.

Peter proclaims to us, the "new" Christians, that we have been healed by the blood of Christ. His words, therefore, make anamnesis of the crucifixion and confront us with the process whereby sin has been undone. If we accept this revelation, it can enable us to live according to God's will. To be specific, the good news proclaimed tells us that whenever, by the power of our baptismal life, we perform actions motivated by that life— actions contrary to the sinful urges of our wounded humanity—we "make present" the example of Jesus and allow him to be Christ our Lord. Then our own wounds, whether they are a competitive spirit or a tendency to resentment, or an exaggerated fear, become glorified in him. They become signs of his healing presence and reveal Christ as a profoundly interior shepherd and guardian of our souls.

Fifth Sunday of Easter

"Do not let your hearts be troubled" (John 14:1). One of the greatest challenges of the first generations of Christians was learning to recognize and to live the *mystery* of the real presence of the risen Lord while enduring the real absence of the historical Jesus of Nazareth. We experience the identical problem. There are times when we wonder, "Is God in our midst, or not?" We would not ask the question, however, if we did not have a deep-seated presentiment of something more than meets the eye. Our own aching hearts point to a "place" beyond.

Jesus lived this mystery before us; this is why he can read the human heart so well. Jesus has been in our position. He understands how our deepest longings can become hidden under a welter of ambitions, anxieties, uncertainties, and whatever else saps our energy and clouds our vision. In today's Gospel, then, when he speaks of "dwelling places," Jesus touches our longing to feel safe in the embrace not only of loved ones but of *the* loved One. Today's celebration helps us recognize that our deepest desire is to be in loving relationship with the Father, and it calls us to turn to Jesus to lead us there.

Gospel: John 14:1-12

In today's Gospel, taken from the last discourse of Jesus, we see how Jesus is aware of his own identity and his mission to his disciples. He knows their desire to be with him, to know him more fully. He is our goal also, and he is our "Way" to the Father. Thus when we hear the words, "You know the way that leads where I go," we recognize the play on the word *way*, and we have time to allow this first inkling of what Jesus is about to reveal to resonate deeply within our entire being. Thomas expresses our uncertainty when he says, "Lord, . . . we do not know where you are going. How can we know the way?" The doubt that human uncertainty interposes becomes the occasion for Jesus to reveal another thrilling aspect of his identity. He not only points the way to the Father, nor even simply opens up a way, but he himself becomes the way to life in God.

The certainty that Jesus is personally *our* way and *our* truth and *our* life allows us to express our longing for God. The Philip in us verbalizes our desire: "Show us the Father." Through the words of the Gospel, the risen Lord, who is always present when the Word is proclaimed in the assembly, reveals to us that his identity and his mission are one and the same. As Son he reveals the Father; as Savior he calls humankind into loving relationship with the Father. Again, Jesus dwells on the interpersonal reality. "Do you not believe that I am in the Father and the Father is in me?" Only persons can be inside each other without losing their identity. Jesus reveals that the communion between Father and Son is so intimate that Jesus can affirm that the Father is accomplishing every work that Jesus himself is doing. At the same time, Jesus calls us to enter into this same mystery (a divine-human reality) of allowing the Father to work his works in us and through us: " . . . the man who has faith in me will do the works I do . . . ." Such is our sublime vocation as Christians. The risen Lord takes us beyond the strained certainty provided by the keeping of laws or the maintenance of structures and raises us, in union with himself, directly to the right hand of the Father. Thus we come to *know* in faith the real presence of God-in-Christ in our midst, and even within our hearts.

Second Reading: 1 Peter 2:4-9

The Second Reading uses a different metaphor to demonstrate how we maintain our identity and at the same time find our fulfillment in union with others. Peter gives us an insight into our being one Body in Christ when he calls us living stones. Since Jesus was himself a stone rejected by the builders, we can expect to share in his rejection. Now, Jesus is the chief cornerstone, approved and precious in God's eyes.

Many Christians find it difficult to deal with the mystery of evil which still rejects Christ the cornerstone. Those who reject Christ stumble over him, but no one can ignore him. Through faith, Christians are privileged to be a chosen race called to witness to the "'glorious works' of the One who called…[us] from darkness into his marvelous light." Our mission flows from our identity. Because we live the life of Christ, we share his mission; when we proclaim God's "glorious works," we make them present.

First Reading: Acts of the Apostles 6:1-7

This mission becomes very concrete in our lives. One incident of such concretizing the Mystery of Christ is related in today's First Reading. Whenever a kind of insensitivity or a sense of one-upmanship develops because of differences in languages or any other human deficiency, then *agape* or Christ-love seeks to find a way to bridge the chasm that has opened up. The First Reading recounts how the early Church chose seven men to take care of the needs of the neglected poor. The mission of these faithful and Spirit-filled men had the same divine origin as the apostolic mission. Works of service or charity (diaconal tasks), in other words, have the same divine motive power as does preaching the Word (apostolic task). It matters not, therefore, in what capacity we labor. The same Lord is the inner urging enabling us all to work together as members of his Body.

Responsorial Psalm: Psalm 33:1-2, 4-5, 18-19

The Responsorial Psalm helps us become even more aware of our Christian dignity: "Lord, let your mercy be on us, as we place our trust in you." Uncertainties and lack of faith surface in every age and in every section of society. The psalm urges us, however, to praise the Lord's trustworthiness, and it assures us that Jesus Christ in the Spirit will continue to help us find solutions to problems that could otherwise disrupt the bond of union in his Body.

> See, the eyes of the Lord are upon those who fear
>   him,
> upon those who hope for his kindness,
> To deliver them from death
> and preserve them in spite of famine.

Sixth Sunday of Easter

When we celebrated the Paschal Sacraments during the Easter Vigil, we successfully passed through an "identity crisis." We now realize more fully *who we are*. Today we focus on the fulfillment of what was proclaimed to us in the first reading of the Vigil: that we have been created in the image and likeness of God (see Gen. 1:27). On this Sunday we contemplate our essential dignity, and we do so not in a detached, intellectual sort of way. Rather, we celebrate what we experience in faith. Today's Liturgy of the Word discloses the particular character of our celebration.

Gospel: John 14:15-21

This Gospel continues John's account of Jesus' farewell address to his disciples and to us. In it he promises to send another paraclete "to be with you always." The Spirit of truth is the abiding presence whom the disciples (we) will be able to recognize "because he remains with you and will be within you." The Holy Spirit reveals that Jesus' departure (his death and resurrection and ascension) brings about the mutual indwelling of the Father, Jesus, and the disciples: "On that day you will know that I am in my Father, and you in me, and I in you." In the Gospel we make memorial of the truth that we are *more than* law-abiding members of the Church whom God rewards for keeping rules.[8] In fact, our ability to obey Christ's commandments rests on an inner power that flows from our existential relation to the Father by reason of the Holy Spirit's abiding presence. The acclamation before the Gospel, taken from John 14:23, explains this ability and relatedness: "If anyone loves me, he will hold to my words, and my Father will love him, and we will come to him."

Indeed, to hold to his words, to say yes to his gracious offer, bewildering as it is, is all we can do. Our Christian awareness tells us that even now we possess a life that transcends the world of phenomena. That awareness finds voice in statements such as "I know that there is a heaven" or "I couldn't live with this suffering if I couldn't pray" or "Someday God will show me where this fits into his plan." In the words of today's Gospel, Jesus reveals the meaning of such statements and shows that they find their source and motivation in nothing less than the abiding presence of the Spirit of truth, given to us by Jesus and his Father.

Love is the most intimate union that persons can experience. When lovers hold their beloved in their hearts, they come to know a mutual indwelling, and in the deep center of their beings they recognize each other. That experience of friendship as a being-in-one-another without losing personal identity attains its truest and most complete expression in the indwelling presence of the Spirit, the Paraclete: " . . . you can recognize him because he remains with you and will be within you."

The primitive Christian communities recognized the risen Lord as an *abiding* presence. Jesus' words "I will not leave you orphaned; I will come back to you" express this abiding presence clearly. It is because of the world's lack of faith that it "will see [him] no more." These words are important to all of us, for there are times when we recognize areas of our lives that are not open to the light of faith. We are not always able to recognize as life-giving what God offers us. But when by the gift of the Holy Spirit we love Christ, then we come to *know* that we are *in him*. Being in Christ helps us, in turn, to realize the truth that we are loved by our Father. Thus mutual indwelling increases our recognition, and increased recognition leads to fuller expression of love.

First Reading: Acts of the Apostles 8:5-8, 14-17

Acts recounts the story of Philip proclaiming the Messiah. His proclamation had power to drive out demons and to heal the sick. Joy broke forth—even "to fever pitch." Such joy is evidence that Philip's listeners' sins were forgiven (see John 20:20), and it also implies that Philip had baptized them (see Acts 2:38). Later, Peter and John were sent to complete the initiation by praying for the coming of the Holy Spirit and by the laying on of hands.[9] The proclamation of this reading recalls the mysteries we celebrated at the Easter Vigil and celebrates the way we live out our initiation into the abiding presence of the Spirit during the Fifty Days and throughout our lives.

Responsorial Psalm: Psalm 66:1-3, 4-5, 6-7, 16, 20

"Let all the earth cry out to God with joy." The "fever pitch" of joy that mounted in Samaria is ours today as we realize that the entire universe has been brought into the saving power of God. The wonderful works of God that we laud in verses chosen from Psalm 66 include both those of creation and those of redemption. In fact, the psalm implies that God orders the course of natural creation to accomplish redemption. It is no wonder that our joy runs so high

Second Reading: 1 Peter 3:15-18

The Second Reading gives us a realistic description of what being a Christian entails. Our initiation into Christ does engender unshakable hope, hope that will express itself gently. But Christian initiation does not guarantee that there will be no further suffering in our lives. In fact, we can expect to have suffering from two sources: from those who libel us for acting in accordance with our new life direction, and from the weakness of our own flesh, i.e., from the conflicts emanating from those areas where we have not as yet allowed the once-for-all death of Christ to penetrate our motives. The Second Reading ends with the assurance that the death of Jesus means our further identification with him in putting to death the "old" life and allowing the fuller life of Christ deep within our spirit to permeate ever further into our entire being.

The scripture readings of this Sunday already concentrate heavily on the function of the Holy Spirit as Comforter. This is part of the awareness that has been growing within the Church since the beginning of the Fifty Days. Continued reflection has brought the recognition that the Holy Spirit is indeed the source of its life and growth. In the power of the Spirit, Jesus reveals the most intimate relationship open to human beings, one that partakes of the very nature of the relationship between Father and Son. "On that day you will *know* that I am in my Father, and you in me, and I in you" (John 14:20; emphasis mine). Such awareness of our identity is well beyond our rational powers; we can grasp it only with the heart in contemplation.

First Reading: Acts of the Apostles 1:1-11

It is important for us to realize that the celebration of
the Ascension of our Lord is much more than the commemoration of an historical event such as Columbus
Day, for example. The time immediately following the
resurrection was unique in all of history. The appearances of the glorified Lord impressed the disciples, but
they could not clearly understand them or absorb their
implications very rapidly. As we have it in Acts, the dialogue between Jesus and the disciples clearly shows how
difficult is is for human beings to allow themselves to be
drawn into the future: "Lord, are you going to restore
the rule to Israel *now?*" (Emphasis mine.) In his response, Jesus first of all accepts the disciples where they
are in their lack of understanding. Then he helps them
see that the moment of fulfillment of the Father's plan
can be known to the Father alone. Finally, Jesus reveals
their intimate, personal mission to help bring about the
Kingdom, not of Israel, but of God. They are to be Jesus'
own witnesses by the power of the Holy Spirit who has
been given to them in the Church.

The reality of Jesus' absence in his mortal form struck
the Church more clearly only as time went on. Influenced by the account in Acts, Christians began to celebrate Christ's ascension as a separate feast—apart from
the fifty-day celebration of Easter Time—around the
second half of the fourth century. On the Feast of the
Ascension we celebrate the glorification of Christ, i.e.,
"the manifestation of His divine greatness breaking
through the weakness of the flesh."[10] We also make present his return in glory: "This Jesus who has been taken
from you will return, just as you saw him go up into the
heavens" (Acts 1:11; used also as the feast's Entrance
Antiphon). In our celebration, then, we glimpse again
how Jesus is ever present to us, breaking through the
weakness of still-unredeemed aspects of his Church, and

keeping us aware that *now* in the midst of our helplessness we are to expect him to come again. At every stage of our growth in Christ we need to wait in prayer for God to "give the increase."

Responsorial Psalm: Psalm 47:2-3, 6-7, 8-9

Following the First Reading we respond: "God mounts his throne to shouts of joy; a blare of trumpets for the Lord." In Christ Jesus, God has gained full victory. We know this in our heart of hearts, and we join the cosmic celebration in full faith. God reigns over nature through redeemed human persons. Divine wisdom will direct the use and the productivity of nature when the human beings who use it are redeemed from greed and selfishness. God also reigns over nations when those who govern, as well as those who are governed, are imbued with divine love.

Second Reading: Ephesians 1:17-23

The mystery expressed in Psalm 47 is revealed even further in the words of today's Second Reading. In Paul's view, the act of furthering what God has accomplished constitutes Christian life itself: "It is like the strength he showed in raising Christ from the dead and seating him at his right hand in heaven. . . ." Such awareness of our identification with Christ brings us joy and a sense of wonder. Being one with Christ in his Body the Church gives us both dignity and power. We can never fathom this fully; we can only ponder it deeply and allow it to grow.

Gospel: Matthew 28:16-20

In pondering we discover God using us to go and teach others. Jesus' words "Full authority has been given to me in heaven and on earth" mean not so much the right to command but the inner power to call forth life. Sharing this power calls for the intimate indwelling presence of Jesus: " . . . know that I am with you always, until the end of the world!" We can say, then, that the Feast of the Ascension is the celebration of Jesus as he is encountered by pilgrims still on the way. Since he is himself glorified and present everywhere, Jesus constantly supports the members of his Body in a manner that only a personal presence can accomplish.

Preface of Ascension

The Preface of Ascension is also significant. In three simple lines, Preface II describes the entire mystery of Jesus' presence. By reason of his departure, we enjoy even greater intimacy with Christ than we did during his mortal life:

> In his risen body he plainly showed himself to his
>   disciples
> and was taken up to heaven in their sight
> to claim for us a share in his divine life.
>
> (Sac., p. 427)

Preface I gives a somewhat more detailed delineation of the entire work of Jesus as mediator. The final sentence of the narrative part of Preface I says:

> Christ is the beginning, the head of the Church;
> where he has gone, we hope to follow.
>
> (Sac., p. 425)

Seventh Sunday of Easter

First Reading: Acts of the Apostles 1:12-14

We could call this Sunday "the celebration of quiet and receptive contemplation" or perhaps even better, "the celebration of knowing that we know." As we hear the simple listing of the names of the apostles in the First

Reading, we come to recognize our own desire to be among those who are obeying the Lord's command to await the coming of the Spirit. We are urged to devote ourselves to constant prayer along with Mary and the others of the one hundred twenty. It is that simple and that profound.

Responsorial Psalm: Psalm 27:1, 4, 7-8

Only through fervent and concentrated prayer can we recognize who we have become by means of our initiation into Christ. Through fervent prayer we apprehend the truth that impels us to cry out: "I believe that I shall see the good things of the Lord in the land of the living." The verses from Psalm 27 also express the kind of security we seek from the Lord who continues to be our light and salvation, viz., the security that comes from dwelling in the house of the Lord. This is not a static concept by any reckoning; it implies the inner depth of intercommunion that occurs between us and the Lord. The final verse expresses well what the Christian longs for: "Of you my heart speaks; you my glance seeks." In a contemplative stance we recognize our longing to see God, and by those words we express what is deep within our hearts. Through Christ we dialogue with our Father in the unity that the Spirit effects.

Second Reading: 1 Peter 4:13-16

As Christians we need constant reminding that our way to union is the Lord himself and that, as his disciples, we must follow him to Calvary. That is why Peter invites us to rejoice insofar as we suffer with Christ. "When his glory is revealed you will rejoice exultantly" does not mean we have to wait until the end of chronological time to experience the joy of Christ's victory within us. Rather, in faith we have come to *know* that victory already in the paschal solemnities. Today we continue to celebrate our initiation, and as we gather for the Eucharist we experience victory anew. In our daily lives we also are victors whenever we perform actions through the power engendered within us by Christ. Our hope of victory is an ongoing reality, then, and we are constantly being called to discern both what motivates our actions and what causes the sufferings we endure.

Sometimes there is only a fine line between what is punishment for our misdeeds and what is persecution for witnessing to Christ. The Roman authorities frequently made serious efforts to make it appear that Christians were political offenders and not heroic martyrs giving up their lives in confessing the new life that Jesus brought. The chief priests brought this same charge against Christ: that he was an enemy of the political regime. Today, being a true witness to Christ is no less ambiguous and difficult to discern, whether it takes place in El Salvador or within a capitalistic economic system or within an atheistic communist regime. The single assurance that takes away the shame of suffering is *our* recognizing that we are suffering in the name of the Lord, i.e., by his power. We can rightfully expect that such witness, even unto death, will follow upon the full initiation of the elect and also upon the thorough renewal of that life-in-Christ on the part of the faithful.

Gospel: John 17:1-11

The first eleven verses of John's account of Jesus' prayer at the end of his farewell address are the memorial proclaimed as the Gospel of this day. Although these words witness to what John's audience was experiencing at the time the Gospel was written, the distinctive character of the Seventh Sunday of Easter in our day is also of "something great about to break forth." Our proclamation of Jesus' final words before his great act of passage, then, is more than a memorial of his farewell address. Rather, it expresses that the passage event is a present reality, an event about to break forth in our liturgical celebration.

Today's Gospel begins with Jesus' words: "Father, the hour has come!" We, the faithful and the neophytes, thrill at this disclosure at this time, for we have come to know God's tender compassion again during our recent passage with Christ, into whose life we have been initiated. We address God as Father in our liturgy today, and in the heart of the Eucharistic Prayer we say, in effect, "The hour has come," for we make memorial of that "hour" which brought us salvation. We make present Jesus' passage, his going away, and his return. The Gospel also proclaims a reality that only Jesus could reveal: the mutual glorifying which constitutes the very life of the Trinity:

> Give glory to your Son
>   that your Son may give glory to you,
> inasmuch as you have given him authority over
>   all mankind,
> that he may bestow eternal life on those you gave
>   him.

Our eucharistic celebration draws us into this mutual glorifying and bestows on us a share in the "eternal life" given by the Father in the Holy Spirit. Today's Gospel is a profound post-initiatory catechesis for the neophytes and for us all. It reveals the meaning of the eucharistic celebration and demonstrates that it is the fulfillment, the climax, of initiation.

Chapter ten of the *Didache*, an early example of eucharistic prayer, expresses well what we proclaim in today's gospel:

> We thank you, Holy Father, for your holy name
>   which you have caused to dwell within our hearts.
> And for the knowledge and faith and immortality
>   that you have revealed through Jesus your Ser-
>   vant.
> Yours is glory throughout the ages.[11]

Today, although we are more prone to speak of the intimacy and shared life that happen within a person-to-person encounter than we are to speak of a "name planted within our hearts," no matter how we speak of sacraments, they are personal encounters. Through sacraments in dialogue and ritual activity—e.g., being submerged into water, being anointed with perfumed oil, or sharing a meal of bread and wine—we express our person-to-person encounter with the Lord and acknowledge that God's name truly is planted within our hearts.

"I pray . . . for these you have given me, for they are really yours." These words also express intimacy. When Jesus prays for his disciples, he is bringing them into the relationship that he enjoys with the Father. Once again, the Gospel shows us that we are living out of a deep sense of familial pride. We memorialize this in the proclamation of the words, "It is in them [us] that I have been glorified." Inasmuch as we have accepted Christ, we too share his life; we too are in God's family; we also bear the family name. We are proud to hear Jesus say that though he is no longer in the world, his life goes on through us who are in the world.

The celebration of this Sunday's Eucharist, then, expresses our joy as we taste and taste again the vitality contained in it. In deep prayer, we allow our consciousness to expand in order to allow the Spirit to flood our entire lives.

Eighth Sunday of Easter: Pentecost

The more fully we recognize that the Sundays of Easter unfold the realities contained in the Paschal Sacraments, the more we find this day a continuation of the foregoing celebrations. Although the day does celebrate the Holy Spirit as the life within the entire Body of the Church, the Eighth Sunday is not a special feast in honor of the Holy Spirit, but a celebration of the climax of the Easter passage and the Christian life. Hence we will treat it from that point of view and for this same reason will not treat the Vigil of Pentecost. Others have made such studies, and their work is easily accessible.[12]

When we consider that this is the fiftieth day of our Easter festival, we may wonder what we have left to celebrate. However, the nature of festivity is to grow and build, and the fifty-day celebration does have historical/religious precedents. The Jews celebrated the Sinai event on the fiftieth day after the Passover, and they also tied this event to a first harvest feast. The early Christians adopted this fifty-day festival and gave it an entirely new character by celebrating the Lord's death, resurrection, sending of the Holy Spirit, and founding of the Church. For us, it is important both to recognize Pentecost day as the close, and even climax, of the Easter celebration and also to realize that the Easter harvest has been reaped already.

We would expect to receive choice portions at the table of God's Word today, and so we do. The flavor of that food is enhanced by the occasion being celebrated. This is because the Word of God is always a *dialogue* with his people. Today we Christians are gathered after the intense period of renewal extending from the beginning of Lent until today.

First Reading: Acts of the Apostles 2:1-11

The proclamation from Acts not only recounts a past salvation event but in that narrative discloses what is happening within our community *now*. Considerable dynamism has been building up within us during "the week of weeks plus one day." The Fifty Days have now been completed; we have been readied for the revelation that God is making, for, like the disciples, we are "gathered in one place." The sound of the mighty wind is the infusion both of the breath of God by which we live as descendants of Adam and also of the invincible love that the new Adam breathes into us through his Easter passage. Today the tongues of fire are the culmination of all the personal dialogue God has ever initiated with human beings. They serve to sum up and contain the entire message of the Old Testament dialogue: the burning bush, Sinai, the pillar of fire, the coal that cleansed the lips of Isaiah, and all the rest. They contain especially the message of him upon whom the Spirit rested and who called himself the light of the world. The sound of the wind and the sight of the fire, therefore, are for us symbols of the experience that is being proclaimed: the presence of Christ in the Spirit *within us as a people.* We are the ones gathered together as his Body *today.* This gathering has been going on in a special way during the entire period of the Mystagogia when the "community and the neophytes" have been moving "forward together" (RCIA #37).

Today our liturgical celebration is the *kairos*—God's time—when Christ's motive force becomes as irresistible as the wind and as powerful as fire to transform. The force of that transformation could not be contained within Jerusalem of old; neither can it be pent up in our church buildings today. Now, as then, peoples from all over the world are destined to hear the message of salvation. These words carry a special urgency to us as we recognize more clearly the call to evangelize third-world countries in such a way that the coming of the "Third Church" becomes a definite vision. All peoples are destined to hear the message of salvation, even if this should entail the relinquishing of some of our frameworks of Western Civilization, as the Jewish Christians of old were called to give up some of their accustomed *ways* of worship.[13]

The content of the message is most amazing too. The disciples proclaim "the marvels God has accomplished." When there is a spontaneous combustion—fire and heat and the release of pent-up energy—and bold proclamations issue forth, everyone understands. So far as speech is concerned, this experience is the direct opposite of the Babel experience, when no one understood the other. While the apostles are speaking in the presence of so many different people, everyone hears the wonderful deeds of God, precisely because the apostles "make bold proclamation *as the Spirit prompted* them" (emphasis mine). The message has the power to unite, because the message is the Spirit.

The stance of the apostles on Pentecost is wholly contemplative. They allow themselves to be moved entirely from within. In the First Reading we see in action the divine-human reality that later becomes praise and thanks or other form of acknowledgment[14] in the Eucharistic Prayer. The disciples exhibit this reality. Subsequently, we memorialize it in our liturgical celebration and in our daily actions. In reflection, we discover how acknowledgment draws us instinctively toward commitment. Thus the Pentecost event becomes a clear revelation of the Christian *mode* of being in the presence of God.

Responsorial Psalm: Psalm 104:1, 24, 29-30, 31, 34

The response to the First Reading is one of the most powerful refrains of the entire year. It indicates and keeps spreading throughout the entire psalm something that has actually happened to us during the First Reading: the vitality of the Holy Spirit. The first verse of the Response (verses 1 and 24 of the psalm) simply blesses the greatness of God as visible in creation. The second verse (29-30) acknowledges our complete dependence on God's sustaining power. The third verse (31) in the form of a wish, declares something that has already been accomplished: "May the glory of the Lord endure forever; may the Lord be glad in his works!" It is not that we think we can add to God's essential gladness; rather, we express our longing to be caught up into it. The psalm concludes on a note of hope that our song will be in harmony with God's delight (34).

Sequence

The Pentecost Sequence is another masterpiece of Christian poetry. It is a love song born out of intense mystical experience. As an epiclesis, it recognizes the action of the Holy Spirit in all the aspects of human life. It lauds the Spirit as the giver of gifts and as the indwelling guest supporting our life in Christ. The Spirit is hailed as the inner power enabling us to transcend all human deficiencies—whatever is polluted, arid, or sick, inflexible, frigid, or wayward. Its symmetry of stanzas and melody enhance its beauty and strength, particularly when it is sung antiphonally. The Sequence serves well to say what this climax of the Easter is: an intense living-in-union with Christ by the power of the Holy Spirit.

Gospel: John 20:19-23

We must look at the Gospel next. Although the text is identical with the first half of the reading for the Second Sunday of Easter, it is colored by the occasion of this day's celebration, even as it helps to make the celebration be what it is. We have said that Pentecost is the celebration of the final day of Easter Time, and thus we expect that our celebration will indicate that growth has happened during these fifty days. By displaying an awareness of the presence of the Spirit and also a strong sense of mission, today's Gospel reveals the nature of the mature Christian life.

The proclamation of Christ's peace, his glorified wounds, the joy of the disciples, the gift of the Spirit, and finally the disciples' divine/human mission—all of these witness that God has forgiven and that the disciples have accepted pardon. All of these signal that their hearts are changed. The disciples in turn become signs to us that this change of heart is made present in us today.

The juxtaposition of the two states of the apostles—before and after they received the revelation of forgiveness—makes it relatively easy for us to enter into the story and to recall that it is our own selves as *newly initiated* that we are celebrating. Fear always powers the process of violence, and the worst violence is the kind we perpetrate against ourselves by straining to keep ourselves hidden behind locked doors. We are the disciples who so often grasp at false security in our fear, and we are also the ones who rejoice when Christ the Lord enters our "enclosure" with his greeting: "Peace be with you."[15] Our joy is assured when he displays his hands and his side. Those wounds are now glorified; i.e., they reveal that they have accomplished what the Father has planned for them. They become sacramental signs to us. Through them we come to *know* ourselves to be *forgiven* sinners. We are assured of this forgiveness by the joy we experience: "At the sight of the Lord, the disciples [we] rejoiced."

The Lord's second greeting of peace empowers the softening of our hearts. The Gospel affirms our oneness with Jesus Christ and also tells us that we too share his mission: "As the Father has sent me, so I send you." This is the most profound missioning that has come to us as neophytes and renewed Christians in the Easter Sacraments. It will take much attentiveness and receptivity to allow the impact of that mission to penetrate us.

We find further evidence that the apostles have accepted God's forgiving love in Jesus' act of breathing his Spirit upon them. Earlier we saw that Christ's gesture recalls God's breathing life into Adam's nostrils. But it means even more. In Acts we find that the forgiveness of sins and the bestowal of the Spirit are closely related, if not identical. Early preaching—we heard it on the fourth Sunday of Easter, and it is still with us today—clearly shows this: "You must reform and be baptized . . . in the name of Jesus Christ, that your sins may be forgiven; then you will receive the gift of the Holy Spirit" (Acts 2:38 NAB).[16]

In our celebration today Jesus speaks the creative Word that reveals to us our share in his mission of forgiveness:

If you forgive men's sins,
they are forgiven them;
if you hold them bound,
they are held bound.

With the disciples, we have come to realize the softening of our hearts, and we have accepted God's forgiveness through the Crucified One.[17] Now we are empowered to share in the essential mission of Christ. This is an enabling mission; for when our hearts are unhardened and the lover in us is again freed by divine forgiveness, we have strength to offer unconditional love to offenders. The love we offer is *agape,* or Christ-love. In its strength we can present to the sinner the reality that he or she is loved and therefore lovable. In this way we free the sinner to love.

The mission of reconciliation has been given so completely into human hands that we experience Jesus saying in effect: "If *you* do not do it, it will not happen." Unless *we* carry on Jesus' mission of offering the Father's unconditional love to sinners, they will not be freed from their bondage. On this day of Pentecost, the Church celebrates its prerogative of offering forgiveness to sinners. We realize that in the Church we have "effective— not merely declaratory—power against sin."[18]

Second Reading: 1 Corinthians 12:3-7, 12-13

The Second Reading reveals that the Holy Spirit is the life of the Body of Christ. We are caught up into newness of life, and this new life is the very Spirit of God. By living this life we are enabled to say, "Jesus is Lord." In other words, we now *know* that Jesus is the inner source of our motivation. It is good that, with Paul, we realize just how radically our initiation has changed us. Christ's love power now extends into the inner core of our being, and we know that every ministry is *within* the Body of Christ. It is no wonder Paul declares that all ministries proceed from the same Spirit. The tensions that develop in any age can be overcome when we realize that in Christ competitive rivalry (e.g., between Jew and Greek, slave and free) has lost its power over us and that our differences can become assets, even as various parts of the body contribute to the common good.

Preface of Pentecost

We reflect on the Preface of Pentecost to see how it celebrates in praise and thanks all that the readings have proclaimed, expecting it to release the long-sustained joy of Easter Time—joy that breaks forth whenever people realize they have been forgiven. We have been designating the Lord's Day celebrations as "Sundays *of* Easter." We have just made anamnesis of the Easter event in the proclamation of the Gospel; in the First Reading we have marveled at the apostles' bold proclamations as the Spirit prompted them. However, the current Preface greatly limits the scope of the readings; it is also at variance with much of the spirit of the *Roman Calendar*, published in 1969, which states: " . . . the fifty days from Easter Sunday to Pentecost are celebrated as one feast day, sometimes called 'the great Sunday'" (*Calendar* #22; translation mine). Patrick Regan notes: "The reference to the 'Great Sunday' taken directly from Athanasius (Festal Letter I, 10), discloses the fundamental theological content of the Fifty Days. . . . they proclaim the lordship of Jesus as attested by his resurrection, ascension, and bestowal of the Spirit."[19] Our joy today, then, reechoes Easter joy intensified now by fifty days of celebration. If the Easter Preface sings, "We praise you with greater joy than ever on this Easter day," (*Sac.*, p. 415) then on Pentecost we could expect something like "with joy spread through all the world, the whole wide earth shouts out its delight."[20]

The central narrative of the Eucharistic Prayer is enhanced and colored by the special fire of the Holy Spirit today. Christ's victory over death and his forming of the New Covenant are the source of the joy we sing in the Memorial Acclamation. The final Doxology gives us another opportunity to enter more fully into the Church that is the *unity* the Holy Spirit is constantly bringing about.

Our Amen at the close of the Eucharistic Prayer today is both the crowning point of this year's paschal celebration and our commitment to live out what we have experienced. The eucharistic meal, too, is our happy celebration of the victory of God's compassionate love, and it is also the food for our continued journey into life. It is as risen Lord that Jesus Christ escorts us into the Season of Ordinary Time in order to journey with us in our day-to-day living. He is present in the abiding presence of the Holy Spirit whom he sent us.

A few considerations are in order at the conclusion of our treatment of the Fifty Days and the Period of Postinitiatory (postbaptismal) Catechesis. There is a noticeable growth or progression inside our celebrations during these Sundays. We move from a kind of overall awareness of our resurrection in Christ to a realization that the Holy Spirit is the life force, the vitality within. We gradually learn how to recognize the risen Lord assuring us that we have been forgiven and that new life has begun; that is, we learn to recognize him in touching his wounds, in feeling his breath upon us, in breaking bread, in being called by name. Ever so slowly we come to *know* that we, the believers, who meet the risen One in faith, live by the Spirit of Christ. This same Spirit is the abiding presence bonding us together in the Mystical Body of Christ. All of this is a continual process of growth; hence there are ambiguities, sufferings, and hesitations, followed by breakthroughs into new life. Thus we can continually realize that "he will come again in glory."

Notes

1. There are obvious ambiguities in the arrangement of the current Roman Calendar. (See *Calendarium*, p. 14, where it names the Sundays, and p. 56, where it mentions the rationale for the length of the Easter Time.)
2. The term *mystagogical* is derived from the Greek and stands for the instructions given after the candidates have been initiated into the Mystery of Christ. Three texts of such catecheses have become well known: St. Ambrose, *On the*

Sacraments, and on the Mysteries, trans. T. Thompson; J. H. Strawley, ed., (London: S.P.C.K., 1966); St. Cyril of Jerusalem's Lectures on the Christian Sacraments, F. L. Cross, ed. (London: S.P.C.K., 1966); St. John Chrysostom: Baptismal Instructions, P. W. Harkins, ed. (Westminster, Md.: Westminster Publishing Co., 1966). See E. C. Whitaker, Documents of the Baptismal Liturgy (London: S.P.C.K., 1960), for sources and at least partial texts. Edward Yarnold, ed., The Awe-Inspiring Rites of Initiation: Baptismal Homilies of the Fourth Century (Slough, England: St. Paul, 1971), also includes Theodore of Mopsuestia.

3. See Aidan Kavanagh, The Shape of Baptism: The Rite of Christian Initiation (New York: Pueblo Publishing Co., 1978), p. 143. Another perceptive view of the "discipline of the arcane" would be to let it teach us that rituals cannot really come into existence before the reality they celebrate has sufficiently matured; furthermore, there is always need for nurturing the ongoing growth in faith. See James W. Fowler, "The RCIA and Christian Education," Worship 56(1982):336-342, especially p. 338.

4. See our treatment of this Gospel as it is used on Pentecost, pp. 206-208.

5. Note that the first part of this reading is a form of berakah.

6. Cf. p. 147.

7. The agony in the garden is the most vivid example of Jesus' suffering such painful emotions as anxiety, fear, loneliness. " . . . he began to be filled with fear and distress. He said to them 'My heart is filled with sorrow to the point of death'" (Mark 14:33-34 NAB).

8. See Robert Taft, SJ, "The Liturgical Year," Worship 55 (January 1981):16ff " . . . what we do in liturgy is exactly what the New Testament itself did with Christ: it applied him and what he was and is to the present."

9. Tertullian, De Resurrectione, 8, has an interesting comment about the meaning of the gesture of extending the hands: caro manus impositione adumbratur, ut et anima Spiritu illuminetur; "The flesh [body] is overshadowed by the extension of a hand so that the soul may be illumined." Causing a shadow to fall (by the laying on of hands) upon the one being confirmed demonstrates a sensitivity to the presence of God that overshadows everyone.

10. For this definition of glorificare, see A. J. Vermeulen, The Semantic Development of Gloria in Early-Christian Latin

(Nijmegen: Dekker en Von de Vegt, 1956), p. 195; see also Ellebracht, *Remarks*, p. 11.

11. *Didache*, translated from J. P. Audet, *La Didaché, Instructions des Apôtres* (Paris: Librarie Lecoffre, 1958), p. 398.

12. See: Martimort, *L'Eglise*, pp. 720-722; Patrick Regan, OSB, "The Fifty Days . . .", pp. 194-218, gives a thorough description of the process by which Pentecost took on the character of a solemnity.

13. For insights about the Church of the future see, for example, Walbert Bühlmann, *The Coming of the Third Church* (Maryknoll, N.Y.: Orbis Books, 1978); Karl Rahner, SJ, *The Shape of the Church to Come* (London/New York: Crossroad, 1974), and *Concern for the Church*, Theological Investigations, vol. 20 (New York: Crossroad, 1981), particularly pp. 77-186.

14. See pp. 147 and 184.

15. There is no verb in the Greek or Latin form of the greeting *Pax vobis*. Considering the circumstances and the acute consciousness of the first Christians that they *already* possessed divine salvation, we can expect the greeting to mean: "Peace is yours," or "You have peace," or "Peace is my gift to you," instead of a mere wish: "May peace be with you."

16. An ancient oration used originally as the Collect for the Tuesday within the Octave of Pentecost reads in part: *Adsit nobis . . . virtus Spiritus Sancti: quae et corda nostra . . . expurget . . .* "May the power of your Holy Spirit be present to purify our hearts." This indicates the close relationship between the Holy Spirit and the forgiveness of sins.

17. Sebastian Moore, *The Crucified Jesus Is No Stranger* (New York: Seabury, 1977), p. 90. See also Schillebeeckx, *Jesus*, pp. 379-397.

18. Raymond E. Brown, *The Gospel According to John*, vols. 20-21, Anchor Bible 29A (New York: Doubleday and Co., 1970), p. 1044.

19. Today's celebration not only brings to a close the celebration of the Season of Easter, properly so called; it also marks the finale of the journey that we began with Jesus when we went with him into the desert of temptations on the First Sunday of Lent. Today's Preface (*Sac.*, p. 429) does us a disservice vis-à-vis the fuller celebration of the Easter Time indicated by other parts of this day's liturgy.

Patrick Regan, OSB, "The Fifty Days and the Fiftieth Day," *Worship* 55 (May 1981):194-218, illustrates perceptively the confusion exhibited even in the *Roman Calendar* over Pentecost as the celebration of the Fiftieth Day of Easter and Pentecost as a special feast of the Holy Spirit, the "Birthday of the Church."

20. My paraphrase of the last two lines of the former Preface for Pentecost:

Quapropter profusis gaudiis,
totus in orbe terrarum mundus exsultat.

EPILOGUE

This book has not attempted to formulate a definition of conversion into Christ in the hope of being able to put it into a category. Neither has our aim been to describe our present-day celebration of Lent, the Paschal Triduum and Easter Time as the privileged forum of spiritual renewal. Nor has our prime concern been to place the RCIA into its proper context. If the book has accomplished any of the above objectives, it has done so only to the extent they have helped us in our primary effort: to recognize and admire, to be open to and enjoy, and finally, to come to *know* that the Christ-event, which we memorialize in our liturgical celebration, is indeed present reality, or more accurately, that Jesus Christ, now our glorified Lord, makes himself present to us as our way to the Father in the Spirit of truth.

The journey into faith is high adventure, even as it is an inner reality of conversion. It involves the entire community-of-persons and engages each person-in-community. We have discovered manifold ways in which God's Word becomes event in the hearts of persons responding in faith. The dialectic of call and response constitutes the mutuality that is the source of growth. To say it another way, we do not try to add a single cubit to our stature, nor to manipulate our relationship with God nor with other members of the Body of Christ; such relationship in faith happens; we are gifted with it.

At this point we would like to highlight just a few of the movements we have traced in celebrating our entry into the eternal plan of God. This plan provides the process in which sinners return again and again to the presence of God, who always meets our resistances with consummate compassion until victory is gained, now in one area of our lives, now in another.

Our identity as created and as redeemed persons is constituted by our relationships with God and with creatures, human and non-human. On the First Sunday of Lent we celebrate our identity with the first humans. Amid the shame of mutual sin, we discover the first ray of hope and victory in him who demonstrated that human beings live on "every word that proceeds from the mouth of God." On the following Sundays we recognize the power generated within our persons by the privilege of our being chosen to be adopted children in the Son, in whom the Father found delight. With the Samaritan woman we recognize the change within our hearts as Christ the Messiah dialogues with us. In celebrating the victory of the man born blind, we not only learn which relationships (in his case, those with his parents and with the leaders of the synagogue) collapse in the face of a call to faith; we also learn that Christ alone is the one in whom we believe. With Lazarus we recognize how sin brings death, but we learn especially that Jesus restores life—yes, gives new life. The liturgy of Passion (Palm) Sunday has two faces, as it were: It assures us of victory, and it strengthens us to make the radical choice to follow Christ all the way to death.

As it has been arranged by the Calendar of 1969, the Triduum is the Church's annual anamnesis par excellence. In it we keep memorial of Jesus' Easter passage in the most solemn fashion. At the very heart of Triduum, as its climax and crowning feature, the Church celebrates the Sacraments of Initiation. In baptism we celebrate the mystery of becoming members of the faith community. In confirmation we celebrate the mystery that is the source of our bonding in the Body of Christ. In the Eucharist we celebrate being admitted to the mutuality of the family meal where we are nourished by the sacrament of Christ's death and rising. Easter Sunday, again, serves a double function: It provides a channel through which the consummate joy of the Vigil can overflow, and it leads us into the celebration of the Fifty Days.

Our faith journey does not end there. We have seen, as we moved through the successive Sundays of Easter, that we celebrate various aspects of the mystery of redemption: that we are forgiven sinners[1] (Second Sunday and Pentecost Sunday); that we discover the risen Lord in our daily lives[2] and in our sacramental celebrations (Mary Magdalene, Thomas, the disciples of Emmaus—First, Second, and Third Sundays of Easter); that the risen Lord *knows* us and we *know* him (Good Shepherd, Fourth Sunday); that Christ is our *way* to the Father (Fifth Sunday); that we are caught up into the intimacy of Trinitarian unity (Fifth and Seventh Sundays); and that all of this happens in the love that is the Holy Spirit, the Spirit of Christ, the Lord.

We have asserted several times in the course of this book that conversion into Christ is a constantly growing reality and that initiation and renewal assume distinctive shape in the Church's annual celebration of Lent-Triduum-Easter Time. Each year we set out anew on our journey into faith, spurred on by the presence of catechumens and carried forward by the series of intense moments, the rites celebrated along the way.

If we wish to experience the joy of *living* the mystery of Christ, we need constantly to remind ourselves that the mystery itself fashions the structures that facilitate its functioning. Thus it would be to no avail were we, at this point, to make a case for whether the Easter Vigil is the climax of the Liturgical Year or only of the Paschal Triduum, or whether the Feast of the Fifty Days begins with the Vigil, with Easter Sunday, or even with the Second Sunday of Easter. It is of the utmost import, however, that we come to experience the inner victory and new life—the Easter passage—that is so great it needs fifty days to express itself.

And now we have come full circle. Jesus, now the glorified Christ, in his Spirit lives so intimately within us and within our memory, which is the continuity of our life, that our response to God is certainly evoked within us by Christ's saving presence. The phrase "And the two shall become one" (Gen. 2:24) is now more true of Christ and us than it was of our first parents.

Sister Mary Alicia Dalton, CPPS, demonstrates that the Christian life comprises much more than a specific spirituality, even liturgical spirituality:

> But one can't follow—rather live—the liturgy daily, year after year, and remain immune to the overpowering action of the Holy Spirit within one's very being. Gradually, almost imperceptibly, the Spirit worked, revealing to me the sacramental power of the liturgy, opening hitherto half-closed eyes and ears to the marvelous reality of Christ's presence in the liturgical action and slowly, surely, evoking in me a loving response to His simple "Come!" Come to the waters! Come and see; come and hear; come and eat. Come, follow me through death to LIFE![3]

Sister Alicia Dalton has expressed well—albeit in a condensed form—what occurs in the liturgy that is the Church's annual celebration of the Paschal Mystery. Upon reflection, we come to know what really happens in the course of interior dialogue. We come to realize, deep within, that our response is itself *gift* from the one with whom we are dialoguing. In the intimacy engendered in dialogue, our answer is evoked *from within us.* All of this expresses the eschatological character of our lives, i.e., that we transcend our current condition again and again and become more fully who we truly desire to be.

We have noted over and over in the preceding pages that conversion/initiation, renewal, and new life is evoked within the celebrating community and its members when it/they are contemplatively aware of and give assent to the dialogue initiated by our compassionate God. The growth that entails the consistent transcending of one's own current level of maturity can never be caused by a technique nor by a studied style of responding. But simple acknowledgment in faith leads to admiration and awe; and these, in turn, are expressed in praise and thanks. In contemplation we come to *know* the presence of the Holy Spirit bringing about the increase of life. This new life is a bonding, a union between persons that calls forth the mutuality that is uniquely free and personal.

Thus we see that the adventure of setting out with and in Christ to undertake his Easter passage with him brings us into that more wonderful condition to which we have been called by baptism. We can indeed affirm that the liturgy "is the outstanding means whereby the faithful may express in their lives, and manifest to others, the mystery of Christ and the real nature of the true Church" (L #2).

We conclude with words from Odo Casel, OSB:

> The content of the mystery of Christ is the person of the god-man and his saving deed for the church. . . .

And again:

> The Christian thing, therefore, in the full and primitive meaning of God's good Word, or Christ's, is not as it were a philosophy of life with religious background music, nor a moral or theological training; it is a MYSTERIUM as St. Paul means the word, a revelation made by God to man through acts of god-manhood, full of life and power. . . .[4]

Notes

1. Sebastian Moore, *The Crucified Jesus*, p. 109, makes the striking statement: "The resurrection . . . is the hatching of man-the-lover out of the millennial cocoon of man-the-sinner."

2. For a clear expression of the relationship between daily living and the liturgical celebration, and also of the integration of the contemplative with the active aspects of human life, see Barbara Doherty, *I Am What I Do: Con-*

templation and Human Experience (Chicago: Thomas More Press, 1981).
3. Sister Alicia Dalton, CPPS, "The Spirit and the Bride Say, 'Come!'" *The Spirit and the Bride* 7 (1981):4.
4. *The Mystery of Christian Worship,* ed. Burkhard Neunheuser, OSB (Westminster, Md.: Newman Press, 1960), pp. 12, 13.